Olesya Khromeychuk

A Loss:
The Story of a Dead Soldier Told by His Sister

UKRAINIAN VOICES

Collected by Andreas Umland

31 *Ildikó Eperjesi, Oleksandr Kachura*
    Shreds of War. Vol. 2
    Fates from Crimea 2015–2022
    With a foreword by Anton Shekhovtsov and an interview of
    Oleh Sentsov
    ISBN 978-3-8382-1780-2

32 *Yuriy Lukanov, Tetiana Pechonchik (eds.)*
    The Press: How Russia destroyed Media Freedom in
    Crimea
    With a foreword by Taras Kuzio
    ISBN 978-3-8382-1784-0

33 *Megan Buskey*
    Ukraine Is Not Dead Yet
    A Family Story of Exile and Return
    ISBN 978-3-8382-1691-1

34 *Vira Ageyeva*
    Behind the Scenes of the Empire
    Essays on Cultural Relationships between Ukraine and Russia
    ISBN 978-3-8382-1748-2

35 *Marieluise Beck (eds.)*
    Understanding Ukraine
    Tracing the Roots of Terror and Violence
    With a foreword by Dmytro Kuleba
    ISBN 978-3-8382-1773-4

The book series "Ukrainian Voices" publishes English- and German-language monographs, edited volumes, document collections, and anthologies of articles authored and composed by Ukrainian politicians, intellectuals, activists, officials, researchers, and diplomats. The series' aim is to introduce Western and other audiences to Ukrainian explorations, deliberations and interpretations of historic and current, domestic, and international affairs. The purpose of these books is to make non-Ukrainian readers familiar with how some prominent Ukrainians approach, view and assess their country's development and position in the world. The series was founded, and the volumes are collected by Andreas Umland, Dr. phil. (FU Berlin), Ph. D. (Cambridge), Associate Professor of Politics at the Kyiv-Mohyla Academy and an Analyst in the Stockholm Centre for Eastern European Studies at the Swedish Institute of International Affairs.

Olesya Khromeychuk

A LOSS:
THE STORY OF A DEAD SOLDIER
TOLD BY HIS SISTER

ibidem
Verlag

Bibliographic information published by the Deutsche Nationalbibliothek

Die Deutsche Nationalbibliothek lists this publication in the Deutsche Nationalbibliografie; detailed bibliographic data are available in the Internet at http://dnb.d-nb.de.

Bibliografische Information der Deutschen Nationalbibliothek

Die Deutsche Nationalbibliothek verzeichnet diese Publikation in der Deutschen Nationalbibliografie; detaillierte bibliografische Daten sind im Internet über http://dnb.d-nb.de abrufbar.

ISBN-13: 978-3-8382-1870-0
© *ibidem*-Verlag, Stuttgart 2023

Printed in the United States of America

In memory of Volodymyr Pavliv (1974–2017)

Contents

Foreword by *Philippe Sands* 9

Introduction by *Andrey Kurkov* 13

Preface 15

1   Volodya, Part I 21

2   Theory and Practice of War, Part I 25

3   A Pair of Boots, Part I 31

4   A Wartime Wedding 35

5   *Vertep* 37

6   A Facebook Message 39

7   The Funeral, Part I 45

8   Lenin 49

9   The Funeral, Part II 52

10 Obituary 55

11 *Wizard* 62

12 The Funeral, Part III 66

13 Twenty-Five Folders 75

14 Masha 80

15 A Pair of Boots, Part II 90

16 Volodya, Part II..93

17 Mama 97

17 *Harvest*..105

19 That Short Story Was So Hard to Write 109

20 Theater of War 114

21 Ignoble Pain..122

22 *Heart* 126

23 Theory and Practice of War, Part II 131

24 The Safest Place in the Army 138

25 Cozy Grave..147

26 *Spring*..157

27 The Flat. Your Flat..161

28 What Remains...166

29 The Enemy...169

30 An Opportune Moment..................................176

31 I Can't Believe You're Dead: A Letter 184

Author's Acknowledgments................................190

Foreword

My generation believed war in Europe was over. We had read of it in distant lands, including the proxy wars fought by leaders in the name of our security. We had experienced local acts of murderous violence, characterized as terror, like The Troubles in Northern Ireland, or the attacks of September 11th, a day on which I happened to be in New York. We had watched the collapse of the former Yugoslavia. But the horror of a full-scale war — of armies on the march, of international borders crossed by tanks, of blockades and aerial bombardments, of prisoners taken and militants executed? No. That, we believed, was a matter of history.

Then Ukraine entered my life. A decade ago, I received an invitation to deliver a lecture in Lviv, at the historic law school. One thing led to another — new encounters, research on the origins of genocide and crimes against humanity, a search for the house where my grandfather Leon Buchholz was born. I find it, on Sheptyts'kykh Street, close to St George's Cathedral, and I am able to imagine a life, his parents and siblings, his departure from Lviv in the summer of 1914. I will learn that his beloved older brother Emil stayed behind, enlisted as an infantryman in the army of the Austro-Hungarians, likely involved in the 'most colossal battle' near Lviv that involved over a million and a half men, described by *The New York Times* at the time as a 'thousandfold, cosmic destruction and wrecking of human life, the most appalling holocaust history had ever known'.

One of the casualties was my Emil, killed in action before he reached his twentieth birthday. 'What was a single murder,' Stefan Zweig asked, within 'the cosmic, thousandfold guilt, the most terrible mass destruction and mass annihilation yet known to history?' My grandfather was never able to talk to me of this loss, not even once.

This tale and others catalyses me into a greater involvement in the life of the city, a place where the lives of my forebears connected with my own work. To delve into the archives, I retain the assistance of two remarkable Ukrainian doctoral students of law, Ihor and Ivan. And then in 2014, war comes to Ukraine. Ihor is called up, sent to the east. The reality of war draws closer. On visits to Lviv, I will see many young men on the streets, in the uniform of active military engagement. I worry about Ihor, my research assistant. Reports of fighting in the east of Ukraine become more acute, so does the rising death toll. War approaches.

The years pass, the fighting in the east continues. Chechnya, South Ossetia, Abkhazia, Crimea, Syria. The lines connect. In the autumn of 2021, I am invited to Kyiv, to deliver a lecture at the National Museum of the History of Ukraine in the Second World War, to donate an artefact from my grandfather's meagre possessions. And then a few weeks later, Russian troops mass on the borders. A full-scale invasion seems impossible to imagine, and then, yes, it happens. Europe is once more at war, in the very places that saw mayhem and death in the times of my grandfather and his brother.

This is the personal context in which I read Olesya Khromeychuk's remarkable, intimate memoir. It is the account my grandfather never was able to write. Not history, but now. Not distant, but proximate. Not imaginary, but real. Here is an account of love and loss, one that is intimate and personal, that transcends time and place, that is brutal and universal, and raises the only question that remains: why?

Philippe Sands

June 2022

Introduction

When Olesya Khromeychuk first wrote this book, along the 270 miles of the Ukrainian border, Ukrainian fighters were under regular artillery and sniper fire from Russian forces and their local collaborators in the Donbas. The ammunition for these continued attacks arrived regularly from Russia, which also sought to make the return of these territories impossible by giving Russian passports to inhabitants of the Donbas.

That war in this book ended only for its hero, Volodya, the brother of the author, Olesya Khromeychuk. He died at the front. He has become a cipher of military statistics. He has also become a treasured memory for his relatives, friends and brothers-in-arms, and he has become this book, which would not have appeared if he had remained alive.

Since then, of course, things have changed. Now, Olesya's book has acquired another dimension. Now it is no longer so much a personal story as the history of a country that has been subjected to the most severe aggression. And this time again from Russia. The new phase of the Russian–Ukrainian war pushes the events of the last 80 years, including the Second World War, into deeper history. Although the new aggression has all the signs of that war of the last century with the massacres of civilians and the destruction of cities and villages. I dare not say that this book is more relevant now than it was when it was written. Perhaps this is not entirely true. But reading such a book during active hostilities, and therefore during the saturation of the information space with war, is an intellectual and emotional test and it is not an easy one. Therefore I am even more grateful to everyone who will read this book now, at a time when one of the largest countries in Europe is fighting for the right to be part of Europe and of the European Union.

With this book, the reader walks the path that Olesya had to travel after the news of her brother's death. It is a very personal story and, I imagine, one that was very difficult to write. But she could not help writing this book, and it is important for people to read it. Her history, the history of her family reflects the history of tens of thousands of Ukrainian families. It reflects the history of modern Ukraine with its problems, hopes, victories and losses. Today, when news about what is happening in Ukraine gets less and less attention in the pages of European newspapers, this book will become an important source of information about the war and, perhaps more importantly, about the impact of the war on ordinary Ukrainians. It does not focus on numbers and dates, but on human experience in a country that has found itself in a state of war.

Andrey Kurkov

Preface

This is a European war that just happened to start in eastern Ukraine. That is what my brother told me, explaining his choice to go back to the frontline in 2017. Soon after, he was killed in action.

Russia's war against Ukraine did not start on 24 February 2022. It started in 2014 with the occupation of Crimea and parts of the Donbas. The reason why the Kremlin was able to escalate it in 2022 was because Russia got away with violating international law and invading a sovereign state unpunished. The world responded with little more than 'deep concern' to campaigns of aggression and terror conducted by Russia for eight years in Ukraine. Vladimir Putin felt emboldened by the West doing business as usual, and the revenue from oil and gas financed not only the continuation of the war, but also its escalation to a full-scale invasion.

After 24 February 2022, Ukraine dominated media headlines all over the world. Outlets in the English language finally got the spelling of Ukrainian cities right, at least symbolically releasing the country from the Russian imperial embrace. The Ukrainian president became a household name all over Europe, and the high streets of cities and towns were painted blue and yellow. There were many Ukrainian flags and supportive posters in the windows of residential houses, which were particularly heart-warming as they demonstrated an overwhelming sense of solidarity among the peoples of different countries of Europe who felt the pain of Ukrainians. People expressed their concern by generously donating to humanitarian causes and opening their homes to Ukrainians displaced by the war. Flags were also flying on official buildings, signifying each state's support for Ukraine, and demonstrating unity against the invasion that the Kremlin had not expected. But if the ordinary citizens were quick to offer practical support, their political leaders didn't always rush to help Ukraine by supplying weapons, introducing sanctions against the aggressor or showing support through other means that could be perceived as politically unpopular. Russia's war aimed to destroy Ukraine, but it was also testing the rest of the democratic world's commitment to opposing imperialism and oppression.

The West was discovering Ukraine. And, as has often been the case with the Western world, it was discovering something that in actual fact had been in existence for centuries. As a historian with something of a public profile, I was contacted by numerous journalists asking me to comment on Russia's invasion of Ukraine. The motivation was often the first question they wanted to discuss: 'Putin says that Ukrainians and Russians are the same people. Is there any validity to that claim?' asked the ones who tried not to offend. 'Are you yourself Russian or Ukrainian? Ukraine was part of Russia once, right?' asked others who did not mind displaying their ignorance. In both cases, the journalists were trying to demystify Putin's version of history. Yet by choosing to discuss the false vision of Ukraine that one dictator has imposed on the rest of the world, stuck in the framework proposed by the Kremlin, they were learning what Putin got wrong about Ukraine, but not necessarily what Ukraine actually was. Few journalists understood that Putin's statements on Ukrainian history, culture or language were simply a weapon of war. Once he had denied Ukraine's existence in words, he proceeded to attack it with tanks and bombs.

It was only when Putin began to do everything he could to destroy Ukraine as a state that the world really woke up to the fact that Ukraine is the largest country within Europe. When Ukrainians, displaced by Russian bombs, started to flood EU cities, the world realized that the country it thought of as 'small' had a population of over 40 million, and several million of those people were now heading west. When the Russian troops started to commit horrific war crimes, the world began to see what the 'Russian world' propagated by the Kremlin really looked like. It looked like the mass graves in Irpin and Bucha. It looked like Mariupol, razed to the ground by Russian shelling. It took Russophone Ukrainians standing in front of Russian tanks with nothing but blue-and-yellow flags for the world to understand that Putin's lies about a 'divided Ukraine' were simply that— lies. These lies had been amplified by the world's media and passively consumed by many of us for years.

For years we also said 'never again' while commemorating the dead of the Second World War. But what did we really mean by that? When my brother was killed, most west Europeans did not even remember that there was a war raging in Eastern Europe. Instead, the international community was preoccupied with the destruction of the Russian opposition by Putin's regime. Few commented on the fact that the leader of this opposition compared the illegally occupied Crimea to a sandwich that cannot be passed back and forth, thereby accepting the grab of Ukrainian territory as a modern-day *Anschluss*. Some Europeans focused on their guilt for Russia's losses in the Second World War, conveniently forgetting that 'Soviet' does not equate to 'Russian', and that during the Second World War, Ukrainians suffered Nazi and Soviet occupations.

Seven decades after the Second World War, when the sovereignty of Ukraine was once again denied by an irredentist state, Russia, the aggressor continued to be perceived as an ally and a victim in World War II, and the world continued to turn a blind eye to its aggression, both historic and current. 'Never again' did not seem to apply when it came to preventing the war in Ukraine.

For years Ukrainians have been asking to be taken seriously, not as a territory in Russia's sphere of influence (have we forgotten what happened last time Europe was split into spheres of influence?), not as just another portion of a 'post-Soviet' blur (will we still refer to that region as 'post-Soviet' in another three decades?). Ukrainians were asking to be taken for what they were: citizens of a sovereign, democratic, European nation with a complex history, diverse identity, somewhat chaotic politics, but a clear vision of the future in which freedom to choose its own destiny was worth fighting and dying for. Ukrainians only won the trust of the democratic world after months of shedding blood in an all-out war and relying on little more than their own defiance.

My brother was killed at the front at a time when the world was cautious to trust Ukrainians, tolerated Russia's propaganda, and did not wish to risk losing economic comforts for the sake of the freedom of a nation somewhere in the 'post-Soviet' space. His was one of 14,000 lost lives that went unnoticed by many outside Ukraine. I wrote much of this book before the full-scale invasion of Ukraine. I wrote it to use the privilege that living in Western Europe gave me to remind the world that our freedom is just as fragile as that of our fellow Europeans in Ukraine, not to mention those parts of the world outside of Europe that usually don't make it onto our emotional or political radars at all. I wrote it because I understood that if we do not help Ukrainians fight for their freedom, sooner or later we will have to fight for our freedom too.

I did not take much notice of my brother's warning in 2017, just before he was killed in the Donbas. In February 2022, as Russia staged a full-scale invasion of Ukraine, I thought of it every day. This truly was a European war that happened to start in eastern Ukraine.

One day the war will end, but it will remain in the minds and hearts of those who witnessed its horrors first-hand, those who came so close to it they could smell its terrifying scent. Long after the actual war comes to an end, the war with the demons that have entered us—as witnesses, bystanders, victims, participants—will rage on. The struggle not to let hatred consume us from within will last beyond the struggle on the battlefields, and all victorious frontline battles will be futile if we lose this crucial one.

I wrote this book to battle my own demons: grief, resentment, fear. I wrote it in an attempt to make sense of a loss: a combat loss that was just one of thousands for the Ukrainian Army; the loss of a brother that was unique for me. Committing these stories to paper I tried to escape the darkness of mourning, to relieve myself of the hatred that planted its seed inside me, to try and move on. This book gives a name to, and tells the story of, just one life lost to this war, but I hope that it can serve to soothe other grieving hearts.

Most of the stories in this book report true events, as they happened. Through them, I hope to offer the reader a glimpse into the conflict both in and out of the trenches. Five other stories—the ones listed in italics in the Contents—are about things that I couldn't report on first-hand, because that would require a level of understanding of my brother's life and death that I cannot claim to possess. Think of them as the fog that might impede clarity of vision but without which the overall picture would not be rendered faithfully.

1 Volodya, Part I

Volodymyr Pavliv, my brother, died on the frontline in eastern Ukraine in 2017. He served in the Ukrainian Armed Forces for almost two years before he was killed by shrapnel near Popasna, Luhansk region. He was 42 when he died.

Volodya—that is how he was always known in our family—was the eldest of three children. He was followed by Yura, the middle child, and me, the baby of the family. There was a four-and-a-half-year difference between each of us. This meant that Yura was close to both Volodya and me, having us on either side of him. Both Yura and I played music and did theater, while Volodya was into art and sports. If Yura was the approachable brother, in my eyes, Volodya was always unreachably older, wiser and taller. Now that he is dead, the nine-year gap that existed between us is shortening daily.

I will never be as tall or, perhaps, as wise as he was, but if I'm lucky, I will reach and surpass the age at which he died. I guess, eventually, in a strange sort of way, he will become my little brother. Although it would be fair to say that I often felt like his big sister even when he was alive. It was me who looked out for him, worried about him, and tried to make sure he was okay. He never asked for any of it. I chose to be his little 'big' sister. Perhaps he was being my big brother, but in ways that were not always obvious to me.

When he was younger, without much effort, Volodya looked as if he had just walked off the cover of some teen magazine. Later on, he sported the look of a wandering artist, a man who'd had a few battles with life. And it was only in his final years that I struggled to recognize him: the sharp features of his face became even sharper when framed by a helmet or a bandana, the usual long light-brown hair was replaced by a short crop, the arms became more muscly, the skin more tanned, the green of his eyes became darker against the khaki that always surrounded him. When I look at the photos of him from that period, I have to try very hard to discern a familiar face in them.

When I was a kid, I used to say that if I ever married anyone, it would be someone like Volodya. Later on, I decided that I didn't want to marry someone like him, I wanted to *become* someone like him: smart, opinionated, confident. He was always reading but never wanted to discuss his ideas, at least not with me. He drew beautifully, played lots of sports and had cool friends; or they seemed cool to me when I was a young girl. In my childhood, he meant the world to me; in more recent years, he caused me much heartache. Our shared blood bound us together and turned us against each other.

We grew up in Lviv, a city in western Ukraine, in a region known as Galicia. Lviv is a beautiful Austro-Hungarian/Polish/Ukrainian city with a terribly complicated history, a rich theater scene and amazing coffee. Like both of my brothers, I was in love with that city when I lived there. Like both of my brothers, I left it as a young person. I moved to the UK when I was 16. Yura also moved to the UK, even before I did: he was 17 at the time. Volodya left Ukraine for the Netherlands when he was 24. We each managed our homesickness in our own way. Yura always dated 'our' girls: someone from Ukraine, Belarus or Russia. I ended up studying the region professionally as a historian. I also set up a theater company that staged plays related to Ukraine.

Both Yura and I were happy to pay flying visits to Lviv to drink the lovely coffee and check out a new theater production, but we were usually eager to catch the flight back to London. Volodya, however, always intended to move back to Lviv. The city for him was not just a pretty backdrop for a nostalgic cup of coffee. His relationship with it was much more intense than that. Perhaps Yura and I had managed to fill the void in our identities created by immigration with the perks offered — albeit reluctantly — by our host country: education, employment, freedom of movement, friends from all over the world. Or at least we told ourselves that we had.

In the Netherlands, Volodya worked doing odd jobs here and there, like many immigrants. He married a local woman, and at one point even seemed like he was trying to settle down. But things didn't work out. After eleven years, he got sick of that sort of life and decided to come home, despite having a residence permit that many immigrants dream of obtaining. Western Europe hadn't managed to fill

Volodya's void, so he kept going back to the place where he felt more complete.

I don't really know who my brother was, but I know who he wasn't. He was never a people pleaser, he was not a coward, he was not accommodating, easy-going or particularly polite. After he died, his comrades said he had been fearless. He must have been fearless to go to war willingly. Soon before he died, he said he had become a warrior. I didn't understand what that meant. Why would a thinker, an artist, wish to become a soldier? Perhaps I didn't appreciate what it meant to be a thinker and an artist, or, maybe, what it meant to be a soldier.

2 Theory and Practice of War, Part I

I have been studying wars for over a decade. Violence described in the pages of books, in oral testimonies, photographs, and archival objects always left its mark on me. I couldn't and, perhaps, didn't want to detach myself emotionally from it entirely, but, with time, I became impervious to it. Now and again, I would leave an interview with one of my respondents — veterans of the Second World War — profoundly moved by their stories. Occasionally I would burst into tears in the archives having found a particularly touching letter or reading an interrogation protocol that was particularly hard to stomach. I invested a lot of myself into it, but it was a job, nonetheless.

When the war in eastern Ukraine started, everything changed. I could no longer think of political violence as an object of research now that a brutal war was unfolding in a land so close to my heart, although still at a safe distance to most west Europeans: in 'a far-away country between people of whom we know nothing.' Following it from London, mostly through media reports and videos posted on social media, I was horrified that the words so familiar from my academic work — shelling, bombing, captivity, casualties, war crimes — were now being used in news reports about my home country. I got used to hearing about losses. Heavy losses, actual losses, official losses, loss of territory, loss of control, personal loss. These words acquired a different meaning. They were more real; they were more palpable.

I saw my friends and relatives go to the frontline. Some received draft notices, others joined up voluntarily. My two uncles were called up: one was nearly 60 years old and the other severely disabled. This was a good indication of the level of inefficiency in the military commissariats especially in the early days. I saw London's Ukrainian diaspora growing in numbers thanks to new arrivals. Some young men were running away from the draft. I never judged them. No one wants to die, for one's country or otherwise. I saw my London-based friends grapple with their emotions: they couldn't decide whether they should return to Ukraine and join up or stay put and dive into the astonishingly efficient volunteer movement, contributing to the war effort financially but from afar.

Before the war began in eastern Ukraine, the phrase 'before the war' meant 'before the Second World War' to me. It referred to history, something I knew a thing or two about. Now, 'before the war' meant the past that was just a step behind the present. The peacetime it described already seemed out of reach.

It was disturbing how quickly Ukrainians got accustomed to the language of war: we learned the names of different parts of uniforms, the jargon of army supplies and, of course, army euphemisms such as 'two hundreds' (killed in action), and 'three hundreds' (injured). I sometimes joined my friends who spent days and nights protesting outside of the Russian Embassy, 10 Downing Street and the Parliament in London. The solidarity we felt in those moments made us feel a little less helpless, a bit more hopeful that miles away from home we might be able to do at least something, if not to stop the war, we knew we were powerless in that regard, then at least to draw attention to what was going on at the other end of Europe.

All this time, I was dreading a call from my brother, who had been living in Ukraine for four years after returning from the Netherlands, to say that his draft notice had arrived. Because he had completed compulsory military service as a young man, he held the rank of sergeant. At the start of the hostilities in the Donbas, the Ukrainian Army was in a dismal state, not only poorly equipped, but also with poorly trained personnel. I was sure that his military experience would mean he'd be among the first to get drafted. But a year passed, and he hadn't been called up. Each day seemed like a blessing to me. Until one day my brother phoned, not to tell me his draft notice had arrived, but to say that he had joined up voluntarily.

My immediate reaction was to get in touch with a good friend — a retired serviceman who had barely survived one of his missions when he was still in the army — begging him to have a word with my brother and change his mind about going to the front. Kolya agreed to speak to my brother, phoned Volodya and told him to visit a military hospital where men returned from the frontline were convalescing. It seemed to have the opposite effect to what I and my friend had intended: Volodya became even more sure that he wanted to go to war. There was no point trying to dissuade him.

My brother volunteered to go to the front. It was his choice. I will never know why exactly he joined up. At one point, he told my mother that he wanted to see for himself what was going on in the warzone. I believe that watching others, people younger than him, return from the front dead or injured had something to do with it. Guilt is a powerful motivating factor.

At first, he served as a machine gunner and spent much of his time in the Donetsk region, near the city of Horlivka. Towards the end of his service, he became the commander of a reconnaissance platoon stationed not far from the city of Popasna, in the Luhansk region. All in all, he spent almost two years on the frontline. When he was briefly demobilized between his first and the second deployment, I tried to dissuade him from going back to the front. He listened to my pleas and said that he had nightmares every night when sleeping in his civilian bed. As soon as he returned to the warzone, the nightmares ceased. Maybe if you are living a nightmare, you have no time to dream of it. Or maybe civilian life, with its multiple shades of grey, simply can't compete with the clarity of the warzone: at least there you know who your friends and your foes really are.

So, as my brother went to the war, the war came into my home. Quite literally. My flat started to fill up with all sorts of military supplies delivered from all over the world: China, Italy, Ireland, the UK, Israel, the USA. I had spent the first year of hostilities resisting giving money to charities that collected donations for the army. I felt that the more we supported volunteers who bought the provisions that should have been supplied by the state, the more reluctant the state would be to reform the army, to prevent the robbery of the armed forces by corrupt officials and actually supply it with the necessary provisions — from socks, t-shirts and food to appropriate ammunition and technology. I might have been right in principle, but once I heard that my brother had joined up, I immediately went online and started buying everything he might possibly need at the front.

Packages with uniforms, medicines and other vital items for front-line life piled up as I ticked off the list helpfully written for me by Kolya. I was ashamed that I hadn't given money to volunteers who were collecting the same items for soldiers as I was now gathering for my brother. I was embarrassed about not being able to stick to my principle of holding the state accountable for its actions and ensuring it fulfilled its responsibilities. Writing anti-militaristic texts professionally, I could see myself being militarized privately, albeit unwillingly. I knew my actions were hypocritical: they were no longer based on the political views of an informed academic; they were driven by the fears of a sister. I no longer knew if I had been right in not supporting charities helping the army. I wasn't sure if I was wrong when buying the supplies for my brother. I realized that one can be right and wrong at the same time. That's what wars do to us.

And then I saw my brother in a news report. My friend, Kolya, sent me a link, saying: 'Take a look, 24 seconds in, they show your brother!'

I asked him how he had recognized him; they had never met in person, having only spoken on the phone. He replied: 'Elementary, my dear Watson! I recognized him by the equipment I helped you buy for him.'

How strange it must be to recognize someone by their military paraphernalia. How much stranger it was to see your loved one on a TV screen in a news report wearing the military gear you had bought for him online. As I looked at my brother, so unfamiliar in his uniform, I wondered whether I knew the items I had bought for him better than I knew him.

3 A Pair of Boots, Part I

For months, my Facebook page was advertising dating sites, maternity clothes, theater performances and army boots. Size 8. The algorithms must have thought that I was a single woman of childbearing age, keen on theater and army outfits. They must also have thought that I have pretty big feet.

I didn't blame Facebook. I had spent days looking at army surplus sites hunting for a pair of army boots. Following my brother's request, I was determined to get a pair that would be lightweight, waterproof, black and size 8. I soon realized that army surplus sites sell just that: surplus supplies. That meant that the most popular sizes—8 included—were very hard to find. I considered getting police boots, because they were super light, and I could get them in the right size and color, but they were not waterproof. I found a pair of army boots that were waterproof, black and size 8, but they were heavy, and the last thing you want when crossing the muddy, black-earth fields of eastern Ukraine is boots that weigh a ton even before the mud piles onto them.

After a week or so of inspecting hundreds of pairs of army boots on my laptop screen and not finding what I needed I started to despair. Every day I checked the main sites to see if they had any new additions, but with no luck. And then, suddenly, there they were: a shining pair of Gore-Tex Pro Combat British Army boots. I couldn't believe my eyes! They were waterproof, black, a bit on the heavy side, but, most importantly, size 8! But wait, what's that? The label said: 'Size 8 medium.' 'Oh, God!' I thought: 'Is 'medium' good? What are the other options?' I couldn't face having to give them up and continuing to look for another pair. Luckily, there were no other options available anyway and I thought that 'medium' must be better than 'large' or 'small,' so I bought them. The special bonus for all my hard work was the fact that they were not 'pre-owned,' like most of the other pairs I had looked at. They were brand new. I was very happy: my brother would have a brand-new pair of proper army boots, the envy of the whole company and maybe even the whole battalion! No one else would have such fine boots.

My order arrived pretty quickly. I was glad to learn that the boots were not too heavy. I gave them a wipe, stroked them gently, whispered 'good luck' to them, put them back in the shoebox and put the box in a bag. The bag already contained a full army uniform, a couple of army caps, army socks, t-shirts, a lightweight waterproof suit, a lightweight jacket and trousers, a helmet liner, a bivvy bag, a genuine British army issue poncho, a few other pieces of army clothing as well as medical supplies, a Celox sachet (the stuff that stops heavy bleeding), water purifying tablets, dry food survival packs, and lots of chocolates and flapjacks. Basically, all the stuff that the Ukrainian Army didn't give to its soldiers. There was also an MP3 player with my favorite music. I hadn't been asked for it. I put it there on my own initiative. My mum added a few little crosses on leather cords: 'Maybe he'll give them out to his friends and keep one for himself,' she said.

Apart from the boots, which were a total pain in the neck, none of these items were particularly hard to get. My friend, Kolya, had made a list of the necessary items and the companies that supplied them. Other friends who had been volunteering for some time suggested a few websites that sold these items. So, the process of obtaining all these army supplies was remarkably straightforward. There was only one article that evaded me: I was also hoping to get a bulletproof jacket, but that task proved to be beyond my ability. Bulletproof jackets are, predictably, not so easy to find online. But, all in all, looking at the large khaki bag stuffed with all these items I felt quite proud of myself for accomplishing my own military mission: getting everything necessary to keep my brother warm, dry and safe.

My mother and I took the bag to a man with a van who would then transport it to Ukraine and pass it on to Kolya in Lviv. Before the war, I had only encountered the services provided by the man with the van when my parents sent gifts to my numerous cousins in the Carpathian Mountains and they, in return, sent us dried mushrooms, honey and all those other delicacies from the old country one misses when one gets a bit homesick.

I wondered how the man with the van felt about expanding his trade to include army provisions. Maybe he liked that he could do his bit for the country this way. He certainly didn't charge us much for the bag. Maybe he felt inadequate that, rather than buying these items for himself and driving his van to the frontline, he carried on in his job as a messenger between peace and war. Maybe he hadn't given this any thought at all. Not everyone thinks of this war, and, maybe, that's fine. When we handed our bag over to him on a sunny afternoon on a west London side street, we felt like we were letting go of someone we might never see again.

4 A Wartime Wedding

The list of army supplies I bought for my brother to help him with his life in the warzone was still lying on my desk when a new shopping list appeared next to it. This made my online order inventories pretty eclectic:

- tartan paper napkins (3 packs of 20)
- emergency burn care dressing (pack of 5)
- yellow/blue satin ribbon (5 meters)
- Tasmanian tiger khaki backpack (1)
- table confetti (20 packs)
- advanced blood clotting sponge (25g x 2)
- favors for wedding guests (miniature whiskey bottles x 50)

If anyone saw this list, they would think I was either having a war-themed wedding or that I was getting married in the trenches. This wasn't far from reality: my wedding was to take place just under a year after my brother had gone to the front. And while I was looking for a wedding venue in London, my mind was in the trenches in eastern Ukraine.

There's a Ukrainian folk song for every emotional disposition, especially if your disposition is dark. There's one, for instance, in which one sister reproaches another for being inconsiderate and putting her interests above those of others: 'Your brother is at war / he's shedding his blood, / you're getting married / and he doesn't even know about that.' The song could have been written about my wedding.

From the day my partner and I decided to get married and have a small reception to celebrate our union, I kept wondering how ethical it was to choose a wedding dress, make a playlist and invite guests for a party while one of my siblings was on the frontline. Every night I went to bed hoping that my brother would wake up to see another day. Every day I wondered if he'd still be alive by my wedding. As the wedding day approached, the tune in my head was getting louder and louder... 'Pah-pah-pam, pam-pam... He's shedding his blood, / pah-pah-pam, pam-pam... and you're getting married...' Folklore is a powerful thing.

Of course, I realized that people got married in times of war. Life went on for some when it ended for others. I tried to be grown up about it and persevered with the wedding plans. After all, I told myself, I was not going to have a massive party. I was never a big-white-princess-dress sort of girl. Ours was going to be a small, intimate celebration. But it is precisely on such intimate occasions that you want to see your nearest and dearest. It so happened that neither of my dear brothers were among those nearest at the time: my eldest brother was 2,000 miles away in a warzone and my other brother was in rehab, waging a war of his own.

We went ahead with the party. It was a nice day. It turned out that it was possible to get married while your loved one was shedding his blood. It turned out that it was possible to listen to wedding toasts and think of the trenches at the same time. It's a shame I didn't get a chance to show my brother the wedding photos; I'm sure he would have had a joke or two to make about them.

5   Vertep

When we were little, our parents took us to our grandparents'
village for Christmas. The holiday season teemed with the sort of
rituals that cannot help but engrave themselves in a child's im-
pressionable mind. My most vivid memories are those of the "ver-
tep". The word itself dates back to the 17th century and refers to a
portable puppet theater. Over time, this evolved into a kind of
street theater that told the story of Christ's birth. The peculiarity
of this performance lies in the fact that it doesn't need to involve
professional actors: most villages and many cities have numerous
troupes wandering the streets, all performing their own versions
of the nativity scene. What they might lack in mastery they make
up for in enthusiasm.

This traditional Ukrainian nativity play is not really about
Jesus. Jesus doesn't even have a proper part in it. He is only men-
tioned parenthetically as something that has just happened to us.
The main characters are Death, the Devil, the Angel and King
Herod. There are also shepherds, Roman soldiers, wise men and
other cameo parts. But their role is mostly to highlight, through
their own insignificance, the importance of the first four.

Everyone in the Ukrainian villages wants the vertep actors to
come to their house. Everyone wants to hear the same story year
after year. To see good triumph over evil. Every year, I watched
rehearsals and then the performance of the vertep in our old house
in the village. Both of my brothers participated in it: Yura invaria-
bly played the role of the Angel. My father made his wings out of
plywood and stuck bits of white paper on them that I curled up

with scissors to resemble feathers. Volodya's part was that of the Devil. He wore a frightening homemade mask. It was black and covered his entire face. You could just barely see his eyes, but only if you tried hard. That summed the three of us up: one brother in white, caring and kind; the other in black, unnerving and daring. And I: an observer of the performance, stuck in the middle.

The vertep characters have accompanied me throughout my life, and when the Angel, the Devil, Death and King Herod spin around me in a macabre dance of childhood memories, it is the Devil's black mask that hovers for a moment in front of me. It stares right down into my soul, looking for the black inside me. It petrifies me. I don't want to look. But I can't turn away. I can't move. Until I notice, through the holes cut out in the mask, that the eyes don't belong to the Devil. I know those green eyes.

Volodya played his part in the vertep so well that they kept asking him back every year. Even when he didn't take part in the nativity anymore, he kept the Devil mask. Sometimes he put it on to frighten others. Sometimes to frighten himself. Mostly, he kept it to remember that life is a blur of white, black and red.

6   A Facebook Message

If you have two siblings, and, after one of them dies, people ask you if you have any siblings, what do you answer? Do you say, 'I *have* two brothers'? But that's not true, because one of them is no longer around. 'I *had* two brothers. Now I have one, because the other one is dead'? That is technically true, but it's way too much information. People ask you questions about siblings to be polite; they don't want to be traumatized by your family history.

It was a long time, during which I paused, looked confused and took deep breaths to fill the silence and calm my nerves, before I learned how to answer that question. 'I am the youngest of three children.' That's what I say now if anyone asks.

I am the youngest of three children. The eldest died in a war. Although one rarely *dies* in a war, one is *killed* in a war. When someone joins the army and goes to the frontline, their potential death becomes a very real prospect. Yet there is nothing natural, nothing normal about death in a war. Someone who is fit to serve in the army is surely fit to live for many years to come. He or she is likely to be quite healthy, quite young, able to face challenges—the perfect ingredients for a long life. A sudden death *should* be unlikely. Yet it is to be expected in war. My brother ended up serving for almost two years and I spent almost two years trying not to think that the least natural end to his life was becoming more and more likely.

One day, I received a Facebook message from someone I didn't know, saying 'Forgive my strange question, but we are looking for this person living in the UK' — followed by my mother's name and details — 'Don't suppose she's your relative?' As soon as I read it, I knew that one of those things I was supposed to expect but had tried not to think about had happened. I just wasn't sure which exactly. A severe injury? Capture? For some reason, I didn't really think of death. I looked up the person who had messaged me and saw that they worked at the Ukrainian Ministry of Foreign Affairs. I immediately thought that my brother must have been captured by the other side. I felt sick. Captivity seemed like the most frightening prospect to me. I had heard too many stories of the humiliation, torture and other horrors faced by the prisoners of war taken by the Russian proxies, and I knew how hard it was to free them.

It was a sunny Saturday morning, and I was on the underground in London, on my way to meet a friend in a park. As the train stopped at stations and the Wi-Fi connection reappeared, I got other similar messages: 'Good day. I am from the military unit where your brother is serving.' *Is* serving! So, he must still be alive! I tried to calm myself. 'Give me your number so I can get in touch with you.' I jumped out of the train and ran outside where there was phone reception. I phoned my mother realizing that I had bad news to tell her, but that I still wasn't sure just how bad. I didn't want to shock her so started by saying that 'it might be nothing, although it sounds serious...' I kept thinking of captivity. In my mind I kept going through a list of friends I should contact to try and get more information, people who could advise us what to do to get him out. But my mum interrupted me and said: 'I got a call from a commander. Our Volodya was killed on the frontline.' She was so calm.

I felt a strange sense of relief: so, he hadn't been captured after all! Almost immediately, the relief was replaced by an icy wave of reality.

In movies, when they show you someone getting bad news, the camera spins to help you imagine the person's bewildered state of mind. It wasn't like that. Nothing was spinning. I had a completely clear head: I told my mum that I was on my way to her place, checked the train timetable for the next train to her station, decided whom I needed to call and in what order. I messaged those people back on Facebook: 'My mother has heard the news already. Thank you for getting in touch.' One of them replied: 'We are just on our way to the morgue. Should be in Lviv tomorrow. The roads are bad here so the guys can't drive quickly.'

I began to think how quickly I could get to Lviv. Could I be there before *he* arrived? The busy London train station seemed completely empty; I didn't notice anyone. I texted my friend to tell her that I wasn't going to the park.

It was only when I got on the train heading to my mother's and phoned my father that I broke down. I had to say the words my mum had just said to me: 'Our Volodya was killed on the frontline' — but I couldn't do it calmly, like she had.

When I got to my mother's place, we didn't really know what to say to each other at first. I didn't even know if I should hug her. We seemed to instantly reach an unspoken agreement that we had to get things planned for the imminent trip ahead of us. We had a task at hand that needed to be dealt with. Such moments leave little space for emotions. Maybe just as well.

Minutes before I had arrived, my brother's commander had asked my mother over the phone if she wanted to see the photos of my brother's body as it was found. She said she did. He sent them to her phone just as I entered her flat. The photos showed my brother lying on the black muddy ground. His head was bandaged with a white cloth and red blood was seeping out on one side. Had they put the bandage on while he was still conscious? Did he feel any human presence as his life was trickling out together with his blood? Or was he completely alone when he died? Did he know he was dying? We had nobody to answer our questions. For the time being, we only had the photos. My mum and I looked at them together. First in silence and then wailing. Quietly. Then I booked our flights to Ukraine and went home to pack. My mother stayed at her place and packed as well, and we agreed to meet at the airport the following morning. I was relieved that we were able to get to Lviv just before he would.

What followed was a week that seemed like a bad dream from which I couldn't wake up. I never realized how shattering grief could be, and never thought that someone's death could turn into a Kafkaesque bureaucratic nightmare. I realized how unprepared I was for the event I had been expecting at the back of my mind for nearly two years.

7   The Funeral, Part I

The glass doors opened, and we were met with dozens of pairs of expectant eyes, all looking for a particular pair to emerge into the arrivals lounge. We expected to be met, so paused at the exit, staring at the people who mostly looked somewhere beyond us. My mum hadn't been in this airport for years. She hadn't seen its shiny new terminal, built for the Euro 2012 football championship. She looked so lost, like a child. I knew I had to take charge. I go back to my home town regularly, whereas for my mother this was only her second visit in seventeen years. Her first visit was to attend her younger son's wedding. Now she had come to attend her older son's funeral.

I started to plan the next steps: texting my dad to say we had arrived safely (his health did not permit him to travel to the funeral with us), getting a taxi to the rented flat, a visit to a local shop to buy coffee and bread. My thoughts were interrupted by a group of strangers who approached us and started saying something. The only word that got through to me was 'condolences'.

The people who met us—a woman with a child (I kept thinking that he should have been in bed at such a time of night) and a man in a uniform—asked us to take a seat in a deserted airport café; it was already after midnight. The woman and the uniformed man introduced themselves and started to explain something about the next few days. I really struggled to concentrate, but I knew I had to focus. I looked through my handbag and pulled out a small notepad I normally carried with me on research trips, took out a pen and started to write things down, much like I did when arranging research interviews.

Monday
10 am—morgue on <u>Pekarska Street.</u>
Tuesday
~~11:30~~ 11:15—morgue.
11:30—go to the church. The church of Sts Peter and Paul.
12:00—service.
13:00—<u>Lychakiv cemetery</u>.
Enei or Eurohotel

The people who met us had kindly thought of everything on our behalf, even potential restaurants for the wake: Enei or Eurohotel were recommended as the most suitable options, because they were not too expensive and within walking distance of the cemetery. I had never thought that the words 'morgue' and 'Eurohotel' would be written on the same page in my research notepad.

My notes continued with names, phone numbers, times and places. I have an annoying habit of opening my notepad on the first blank page I find and just starting to write there. My notes, therefore, end up being spread all through the notepad and sometimes written upside down. But in this case, it reflected my state of mind at the time much better than if they had been recorded neatly and methodically.

Liuba. That was the name of the woman with the child who should have been in bed by now. Liuba looked like a woman you'd like to have a drink with: lively and energetic. She was roughly my age and so mature enough to face up to whatever life threw at her and young enough to have the energy to deal with it. Her eyes were those of a woman who had seen pain. If not her own, then certainly that of others. Plenty of it. She made us as comfortable as she could, given the circumstances. Liuba was the one who told us exactly what to do, where to go and whom to contact if we had any problems. She gave me her mobile number – in my notes it was highlighted in blue – and told me that I could get in touch any time. She meant it. I didn't quite get what her job was, other than the fact that it involved helping families like ours, even if this entailed dragging her child to all sorts of places at all times of the day or night. The little boy was patiently sitting nearby waiting for his mother to finish her working day long after it should have been over. As far as I was concerned, Liuba worked as our guardian angel from the moment we stood looking lost in the arrivals lounge and for some months to come.

The man in the uniform was called Oleh. I wrote his full name down in my notes but, in my mind, he remained 'Oleh, the man in uniform.' He was working for the military commissariat. Much later, we learned that he had been working there when Volodya joined up. It was also he who would later present my mum with the Order for Bravery, awarded to my brother posthumously. Oleh was serious and officious. Like Liuba, he may well have been my age, but his stern look and the uniform made him look older. Having grown up in Ukraine in the 1990s, where the rule of law was not respected by law enforcement agencies, I generally don't warm to people in uniform quickly. I prefer to avoid them at all costs. This man, however, somehow seemed approachable. Unlike Liuba, who did all the talking and explaining, Oleh didn't say much. He looked at us patiently, silently and directly. He didn't try to hide his eyes, although this situation was far from comfortable for him. I respected that. These two people made the days that followed just about bearable.

We finished our airport briefing, found a taxi and got to our rented flat. I thought I'd fall asleep out of sheer exhaustion, but I couldn't. I had been told that my brother's body had already arrived in Lviv and I was wondering where he was. My mum slept in the room next door and must have thought that I couldn't hear her. But I could. Now and again, I would hear stifled wailing. Then silence. Then more quiet sobbing. The night passed somehow.

In the morning we sat in the kitchen before heading to the morgue, as written in my notepad. Does one have a coffee before visiting the morgue? There was no question about breakfast. We wouldn't be able to stomach it. I don't remember if we had coffee. I don't remember how we got to the morgue. I only remember meeting my brother, or rather his body, there. That was the first of the three things I dreaded most of all.

8   Lenin

The first thing I thought when I saw him in the morgue was
that he looked like Lenin. He never looked like Lenin in life.
I thought I must be going mad. He had a high forehead and
a little beard, like Lenin in those pictures I saw as a child,
and that must have made me think of Lenin lying in the
mausoleum.

I always envied my brother's high forehead. I wanted
to have the same. But mine was always smaller. I could never hold my head high like he did. Proud. Brazen even. When
we were children, he rode horses, went to fencing classes
and swam really well. I sang songs and acted in a theater. I
couldn't ride horses, fence or swim. He picked up foreign
languages, English, Polish, Dutch, as he travelled the world
just by hanging out with people. I had to study my languages long and hard. He was a philosopher without even
trying. I kept getting one degree after another, but always
felt inadequate in his company. He was a talented artist, and
I couldn't even draw a stick figure. I admired him, resented
him, feared him and always loved him. No matter what.

And now I reproached myself for thinking that he
looked like Lenin.

I was very scared of entering the morgue. I was frightened of seeing the scars, the wounds, the fractures. I had
already read the report of the military medical commission
that came from the frontline: 'Skull fracture caused by
shrapnel. Crushing of the brain. Injuries due to war opera-

tions resulting in death. The injuries and the cause of death were sustained in the protection of the homeland.' I pictured all this in my head in some detail. So, I prepared myself as much as I could for the morgue. But when we entered, all I could think was that he looked like Lenin. It must have been the high forehead.

He looked as if he was asleep. His features were peaceful. There was a very small wound above his right temple. There was a big scar across the back of his head, but it was thoughtfully covered by the pillow, so we could barely see it. His uniform was clean and new. I wondered whose job it was to put these new uniforms on the dead soldiers before they were handed over to their families. The people who did this job were the real heroes. I noticed that the boots he was wearing were brand new and thought that it was a shame for new boots to go in a coffin when so many soldiers needed them at the front. I was cross with myself for thinking that.

I caught myself thinking that I was grateful that we could bury him. So many people go missing in action, die somewhere in the middle of minefields never to be found again; so many are killed in the basements of their captors, and even if their bodies are returned to the relatives, they are not always recognizable. I was lucky. I could say goodbye to a body that looked like my brother.

I held his hand. I stroked his face. I wanted to kiss his high forehead, but I was worried he wouldn't like it. He was never a touchy-feely kind of guy, or at least that's what he wanted people to think.

I stood there and realized that the face in the coffin no longer resembled Lenin. The features were undeniably those of my brother. I looked at him and remembered the time he picked me up from school. He hated picking me up, but I loved it, because when my big brother picked me up all the boys could see, and they would never dare mess with me! I would chat away all the way home. He wouldn't say a word. I don't think he listened. I didn't mind. I forgave him for not listening then.

I forgave him many things when we grew up too. For sending cruel messages when the PTSD got the better of him. For not sending any messages for months. For going to the army of his own volition. For getting killed. I forgave him everything as I gathered the courage to kiss his high forehead.

9　The Funeral, Part II

We left the morgue and Liuba was there again. I was grateful to see her face. It meant we were not alone.

'You need to speak to the priest and buy bread for tonight's service,' Liuba told me.

'Speak to priest. Buy bread,' I wrote in my notepad.

'You can get the wreath for the grave in a shop just over there,' said Liuba.

I would have forgotten about the wreath for sure.

'Get a wreath,' I wrote.

'Have you decided on the restaurant for the wake? They are both nearby. You can pop in and get everything arranged, like the menu and so on, on your way from here.'

'Go to Enei,' I wrote.

I couldn't face inviting people to a place called Eurohotel for the wake, so I opted for Enei. Enei is the Ukrainian name for Aeneas, the Trojan hero of Homer's *Iliad* and Virgil's *Aeneid*. He is also a bit of a comical figure in Ukrainian culture because a version of his adventures was written as a mock-heroic burlesque poem in the 18th century and every school kid knows it, if not from Ivan Kotlyarevsky's hilarious and daring original, then at least from a more recent cartoon version. The poem turns the classical heroes into roving Ukrainian Cossacks who, when they're not getting drunk, are constantly chasing adventures. I thought my brother would have approved of a wake in an establishment named after a roguish but lovable vagrant.

I remembered that the last time I had visited restaurants in my home town and chosen menus was when I was helping Yura, my other brother, arrange his wedding. I was surprised to notice how similar some of the rituals were: talk to the priest, choose flowers, find a restaurant, choose the menu, invite people. A funeral, like a wedding, is a social affair.

'Then you need to go to such-and-such office to get your brother's death certificate,' Liuba continued.

'Can't we do it after the funeral?' I asked.

'No, you need it for the funeral,' she explained patiently.

I wrote: 'Get death certificate. Urgent. Ask Yura to buy bread and take it to the priest.' The schedule was getting too much for me to handle by myself. Yura was with me, and I was glad to delegate at least some of the tasks to him.

When we got to the registrar, a woman in a fur coat, who interrupted her lunch break especially for us, asked me to hand over my brother's passport. I did as instructed. She took it and put it away in one of her drawers.

'Won't you give it back to us?' I asked.

I didn't want to let go of even the smallest piece of paper that belonged to my brother. Especially his passport!

'No, we need to file it,' she explained.

Passports are important in my family. Immigrants become synonymous with their passports whether they like it or not. The little book becomes a ticket out and a constant reminder of your homeland. It becomes part of your identity. When waiting in a queue at a border, you learn to identify other people's passports just by looking at the facial expressions of customs officers. If they smile, the passport holder must be from the EU or other 'civilized states'; if they frown and turn the pages as if looking for some secret information, the passport holder is probably 'one of us,' one of the special ones from one of those poor, suspicious countries, with a passport that can be more of a hindrance than a help when travelling the world.

I wanted to keep my brother's passport. With its stamps and visas, it would remind me of his life in Western Europe, of the many adventures of my own Aeneas. But it so transpires that the passport stops being valid when the person to whom it belongs is no more and it has to be filed away. So, I surrendered it to the woman in the fur coat and got a death certificate in return. It was a poor substitute for the passport; it didn't have a story to tell. Or, at least, its story was not as adventurous and exciting as that of the passport. It didn't seem like the right ending to the story of my Aeneas.

Several more offices, more trips to the morgue and the restaurant, millions of phone calls and another sleepless night later, Monday was finally over.

10 Obituary

When we got back to the rented flat after visiting the morgue, the registrar and the restaurant, I found many messages of condolence on my phone. I also found some Facebook posts that had me tagged. They shared obituaries that had started to appear in the regional newspapers. After I had answered the private messages, I started to read the obituaries.

It turns out that one can learn many things from obituaries. Even things that hadn't happened. Those were, of course, the most interesting passages. People who write obituaries must feel a pressure to make the subjects of their texts as inspiring and important as possible. But, let's face it, few of us are particularly inspiring and even fewer are important. So, their only choice is to make things up, to embellish.

Obituaries for those who have died on the battlefield seem to follow the same template. The first paragraph gives basic facts: so-and-so served in such-and-such unit, was of such-and-such age when he or she died in such-and-such place while fulfilling his or her duty to defend the homeland. The second paragraph is about how human the fallen soldier was. It's supposed to get us to identify with him or her. It could be a quote from a relative or a friend: 'He was a talented artist'; 'She had three little children.' It's usually the kids that are emphasized when a woman dies, not her occupation or her military accomplishments.

'He loved his native city.' That was a line in most of my brother's obituaries. It's true, Volodya genuinely loved Lviv. He couldn't understand why I didn't want to move back. I explained that I felt like I had grown out of it, like one grows out of one's favorite childhood clothes: you still love them and don't want to give them up, but you can't wear them anymore. I explained that the Lviv of our childhood was not the Lviv of today. He saw it differently. I guess, for him, Lviv was whatever he made of it in his imagination.

Like me, my brother lived for many years away from Lviv. Mostly in the Netherlands, but, for some reason, the obituaries wrote that he had lived in Belgium. It only takes the first reporter to make a mistake for all the others to re-print it. Fact-checking did not seem to be terribly important for these obituary writers, so they moved my brother from the Netherlands to Belgium. But what difference does it make if it is one wealthy Western European country or another? To most people reading those obituaries, Belgium or the Netherlands stood for the same thing: the West, a prosperous life, no war and no need to go to war.

Western Europe was a perfect setting for the third paragraph, the one about the heroic decision to go to the front. You need to have something to leave behind in order for your decision to join the army to be heroic: if you have nothing of value to leave—little kids, a fancy job, a cozy life in Western Europe—then you have nothing of value to lose. Apart from your life, but its value is dubious. You may as well go to the front. Nothing heroic about that. So, the third paragraph in my brother's obituary ran as follows:

'For a lengthy period of time, he lived abroad—in England and Belgium. Although he had a good job abroad, he was not afraid to return to his motherland to fight in the East as soon as he could. Because every one of us should take responsibility for the future of our country.'

Or something along those lines.

Now, pathos aside, this would be a fitting paragraph for an obituary. The only problem with it was that almost none of it was accurate. First, as we've already established, he lived in the Netherlands. He visited the UK twice and I don't even know if he ever went to Belgium. Second, he didn't have a good job in the West. Few immigrants do, especially those from poorer countries like Ukraine. Unless your concept of a good job is getting minimum wage on a precarious contract because there's always a queue of other immigrants ready to replace you, cycling 12 miles to work because you want to save on travel and regularly hearing xenophobic abuse from your employer because... Well, I don't know why people feel compelled to say xenophobic things to immigrants who are actually working for them, but they do. But if you leave a job like that, or if—God forbid—you don't have any job at all before you sign up for army service, or if—an even more frightening thought—you join up *because* you don't have a job and army service is a way of earning a living, that's not going to look good in your obituary.

The third, and perhaps the most frustrating inaccuracy was that he hadn't returned to defend his motherland. He may well have done this if he had still been living abroad when the war started, but he had returned a few years earlier. Why? Why do many immigrants come back? Because they get fed up with the life of an immigrant who never fits in, never fully belongs; they get fed up with their name never seeming to come out right when said by the locals, even by those who try hard, even by those who say it with love. Because nothing keeps many immigrants abroad. Because while they are away, they imagine the country of their youth to be exactly what they want it to be, regardless of what it actually is. Because of millions of other very ordinary reasons that have nothing to do with defense of the homeland or heroism.

And, finally, he hadn't signed up as soon as the war began. For some reason, his draft notice did not arrive, although he'd been expecting it to; he thought about his decision for a while — which is a reasonable thing to do when the decision has a potentially lethal outcome — and, eventually, signed up for the front voluntarily. He put his old army uniform on (the one he had worn when he served as a conscript in the 1990s and kept as a souvenir), turned up to the local military recruitment office (the same one where he had been drafted as a young man), and reported that he wished to go to the frontline. I learned all this from the people in the military commissariat much later. My brother seemed to have made quite an impression on them: they all remembered this scene and relayed it to my mother and me enthusiastically when we came to collect the Order for Bravery that he had been awarded posthumously.

So, there you have it: one short paragraph and at least four inaccuracies. The obituaries painted a very unambiguous picture of a successful man in his prime who dropped everything and rushed to give up his life for his native land. I guess I should have felt proud reading it. The only problem was that I didn't recognize my brother in this description. It's not that he wasn't brave or didn't care about his homeland. He was and he did. It's just that things were much more prosaic. And if I didn't recognize him in this description, if he didn't live up to it (or didn't die up to it?), did that mean that I was not to feel proud of the real him because his actual story didn't fit the heroic template?

Oh yes, the template. There is usually some room for a description of a heroic death. Because the loss of a soldier's life has to be described as heroic — not as a tragic mistake, an accident, a disaster, but as an act of selfless heroism. The thing is, there is often little that is heroic about dying on the frontline. My brother's friend, the last person to talk to him on the phone just moments before he died, said that the last thing he heard him say was *'Suka! Bliad'!'*, which can be roughly translated as 'Shit! Fuck!' They were planning my brother's leave, which was coming up in a couple of days, and then he heard some blasts in the background and my brother swearing. And then the connection was lost. Not something for an obituary, right? Something for life, something for death, but not for an obituary.

As I read my brother's obituaries, I wondered: if reality doesn't make it into obituaries, then what does? These inaccuracies might seem like innocent embellishments, a journalistic trick to make ordinary people seem a bit more extraordinary. But why is an uninteresting and unimportant life lost in a war not deserving of a mention in the news? And, in any case, whose life do we consider to be valuable, and whose expendable to the point that it's not worthy of an obituary? As lives are lost in the war in eastern Ukraine, all that is left of them is memory. But what sort of memory do we create for them with our little white lies?

As I read my brother's obituaries, I wondered whether the journalists who wrote them appreciated that another serviceman or servicewoman reading an embellished text and realizing that his or her life was nothing like the one described there might think himself or herself worthless. Whether they gave any thought to what it might be like for relatives to read an obituary and not really recognize their loved one behind all the embellishments. That it might not help and even actively harm the process of grieving.

As I read my brother's obituaries, I dreaded even to think what would be written in my own. But then I haven't left my life in Western Europe to defend my homeland, so, perhaps, I wouldn't be deemed worthy of an obituary at all. Perhaps it's just as well.

Nearly five years later, I got to experience the fitting of my brother's death into news stories once again. In the midst of the intensification of reports about Russia's potential full-scale invasion of Ukraine, I was getting messages from British journalists who were looking for ways to keep their readers engaged in a story that hadn't quite broken yet. They were hoping to speak to someone with a connection to Ukraine, and thus to the war that was 'about to start'. They reached out to me.

First, I had to explain that the war was not about to start; that it had started eight years prior. Then I explained that for some, like my brother, it had already ended when the shrapnel pierced his body. They would listen at first, but as soon as they realized that my 'connection' was already dead, they interrupted me—sometimes offering condolences— and asked if I knew of someone who was in imminent danger at that moment. My story didn't fit the story they were tasked to write. It was old news. They needed to *make* news.

Soon after I had these exchanges with the media, the entire country found itself in imminent danger. No more shortage of suitable stories. Yet as casualties started to be measured in thousands, they too quickly became old news, and the media the world over had to keep looking for ways to sustain the attention of readers whose war fatigue intensified with every death.

11 Wizard

The paths my brother walked before he stumbled upon his final destination were many and each was more twisted than the one before. Am I to believe that whatever road he would have taken was going to inevitably lead him to the same end point? How am I to stop thinking that, had he stayed put in not-so-welcoming but relatively safe Western Europe, he would have escaped the deadly embrace of the continent's easternmost part?

The bright lights of a big wealthy city only attracted him briefly before he tired of them. As with all new things, our excitement for a new place lasts as long as the novelty. Once we glimpse what is behind the window dressing, once we start to understand the meaning of the foreign words we hear around us, once our eyes get used to the unfamiliar faces, we ascertain that the new place differs little from the old and we seek fresh discoveries.

My brother couldn't stand being constantly reminded of his foreignness. With him, it wasn't done in the patronizing way in which I often get exoticized, but in that crude – 'we don't want you here, foreigner' – way. And so he kept walking away from people and places, exploring himself and discovering new paths. Until his path came to an end.

I have often tried in my mind to follow his trail to Amsterdam, where he lived, fell in love, and made art. I have tried to understand how it led him back to Ukraine, to the war. I don't have much to base this reimagining of his life on other than fragments of conversations I recall, and the drawings he left behind. I make up my own stories to make sense of his. Here is one of them.

Once upon a time, there were three friends: the Wizard, the Cat and the Eagle. Or were they, in fact, one person? Nobody knew. And it didn't matter. Even if there were three of them, they may as well have been the same person because wherever they went, they went together. They each performed a function that the other two relied on: the Cat was the one who sought comfort and attachment, who desired to find a cozy spot to call home; the Eagle's job was to see the bigger picture, rise high up and remind the other two that everything below was small and insignificant, including themselves, to keep them unattached. The Wizard was the wise and fearless one. His task was to choose the paths which the three of them would walk.

Once, they found themselves in a big city. They walked from one district to another, along the canals, looking for somewhere to settle. Dressed in his long overcoat fastened with a simple rope, a tall hat on his head and a long walking stick in his right hand, the Wizard didn't look like one of the locals. He rarely looked up from under his hat. Most people could see only his long hair, his beard and moustache, overshadowed by the brim of his hat.

They walked the city knocking on doors and asking if those living in the colorful houses had a room for them. Some said, 'Sorry, my friend, everything's taken,' without even opening the door; others listened to the Wizard, but, hearing his unfamiliar accent, they would quickly shut the door in his face. There were also those who wouldn't even let him finish his sentence and said: 'Why did you come to our city? Go back to where you came from!'

And so they walked on. A long time passed, and they passed through district after district of the big city. Until, one day, they saw a strange settlement on the outskirts that didn't look like any-

thing they had come across before. The dwellers they found in the settlement were a bunch of misfits, outcasts and eccentrics. They included Fairies, Goblins, Elves, Werewolves – pretty tame as it turned out – and a Vampire who had sold his castle in Transylvania, downsized, and settled there after his retirement.

The Wizard knew that they had found the right place. Everyone there had a strange accent that didn't sound like the accent of the locals in the doorways. No one was telling them to go back where they came from. They had all come from somewhere and this was their home now.

The years went by with the three of them happily spending their days in the settlement on the outskirts of the big city. The Wizard found time to return to his great passion: painting. He painted the Fairies, the Goblins, the Elves, and even the Werewolves. The Vampire was the best sitter. He could stay still for centuries if need be.

One day a young local Witch stumbled upon the settlement. Her long red locks brightened the place up. The Wizard even decided to paint her portrait on his largest canvas, and she learned to speak the Wizard's language.

The next line could read: 'And they lived happily ever after.' But that happens only in fairy tales, not in real wizards' lives. In real life, a new path was waiting for the Wizard. It was time to discover it.

And so the Wizard, the Cat and the Eagle set off to wander through ever new lands, meeting and painting many new faces. But if you walk for so long, you are bound to return to where you started. And when that happened, when they found themselves in the town they had left many years ago, long before they discovered the big city, the Wizard decided that it was time for him to make his final work of art: he painted the three of them.

The picture portrayed them just as they had spent many years together: the Wizard in his coat and hat, with a long walking stick; the Cat beside him; the Eagle in flight above them; a long, winding, familiar path behind them. They had just passed a road sign: the sign pointing to where they had come from said 'Life'. They walked on.

12 The Funeral, Part III

Tuesday was the day of the funeral. We followed the schedule we had been given by Liuba and which I had written down in my notepad. We met at the morgue and travelled to the church in the hearse, together with the coffin.

Saints Peter and Paul Garrison Church is an impressive place. Built in the early 17th century in the baroque style, it survived the iconoclasm of the Soviet period because it served as a book depository. Neither my mother nor I had visited the church in the past, as it was only reopened in 2011 when it was given over to the Greek Catholic Church and the Ukrainian military. It was opened on 6th December: the Ukraine Armed Forces Day, and, as it happened, my brother's birthday. Historically, the church had served as the garrison church for the city, and after its restoration it continued to serve the military. The funeral masses for the Lviv soldiers killed in the war in the Donbas take place there.

As well as the gold and the frescoes of the baroque interior, the church contains displays about the current war: a birch cross that had originally stood on the frontline, a large shell casing, photos of the children of fallen soldiers. There were also photos of soldiers from Lviv who had been killed in the war. They were pinned to a notice board that clearly had sections added as more and more pictures appeared. Looking through them, we found a photo of my brother. He was in his civilian clothes, with sunglasses on his head, and his beloved city served as a backdrop. I was grateful for a small blessing; I found photos of him in uniform alien and preferred to see him as I knew him — as a civilian.

We left the car and watched a group of young men in uniform lift the coffin and carry it into the church. I didn't expect that. I thought the whole thing would be a quiet family affair. As they entered the church, I couldn't believe how many people there were inside. I recognized some of the faces, but most were not known to us. It turned out that the city residents came to the funerals of soldiers killed in the east even if they didn't know them personally. The church was full.

The young men in uniform stood guard near the coffin throughout the service. One of them held a portrait of my brother. I could see his face on the portrait and in the open coffin. I didn't know which one felt more real. Neither really looked like my brother. The whole ceremony was very formal. I pitied those young men: what a strange thing to do for a cadet. On the other hand, if they intended to become soldiers, perhaps standing guard at another soldier's funeral should be a compulsory part of their training. Perhaps that is when they can really decide if this vocation is for them.

I wanted to approach the coffin, but the church full of strangers and the young men standing guard made it rather awkward. The most awkward thing, however, was the presence of the media. They seemed to be everywhere: filming, taking photos. Part of me felt sorry for them: how do you find a good angle and decent light, in order to get good footage of a funeral in a gloomy old church? But mostly I felt annoyed. With their lights and cameras, they were turning one of the most intimate moments—a final farewell—into something that resembled a theater show. I knew it was their job, but the last thing my family and I needed was to be filmed as we were being torn to pieces by grief.

The service ended and the second of the three moments I dreaded most of all came: the closing of the coffin. My mum said her farewell just before they closed it, but I couldn't. My legs felt like they were made of lead. I didn't want the journalists photographing our last goodbye. As they were closing the coffin, I wanted to scream: 'No! Don't! Not yet!,' but I couldn't say a word. I just stood there and watched them close it, lift it and take it out of the church.

The next thing I remember is my mother being approached by a man with a massive bunch of white roses outside of the church. I recognized the mayor of the city and dug my fingers into his arm as he was letting go of the flowers. I don't remember what exactly I said to him, but it wasn't 'thanks for the roses'. In return for a photo opportunity with a grieving family and a dead soldier, I wanted him to feel at least a fraction of our pain.

We traveled to the cemetery in a hearse. Sitting there, not far from the coffin, I felt afraid of dying for the first time in my life. Terrified. As we passed the local war veterans' office, we saw people holding a flag that stretched for several meters. That was their way of saying goodbye to one of their own.

We reached the gates of the city's most famous cemetery. It was so familiar to me from my childhood. I liked to
walk there among the old Polish, Austrian, Ukrainian and
Soviet graves. It was always an open-air lesson in history.
My brother also liked to walk there. He even told me a funny story once, about the time he and his mates decided to
visit the cemetery at night. Walking between the graves they
met an old woman. To overcome their fear and show off in
front of the others, one of them asked:

'Which grave is yours, ma'am? This one or that one?'

'Mine is over there, young man,' said the old woman,
pointing at a grave nearby and leaving the little brats in terror.

That story always made me laugh. I remembered it as I
entered the cemetery.

None of us would ever have dreamed of being buried
in the most prominent cemetery in the city. Walking behind
the hearse, passing the graves of famous composers, poets,
military generals and political leaders, I found it hard to
believe that my brother would be among them for eternity.

Lychakiv Cemetery is a curious place. One whole part
of the cemetery is given over to various military burial plots.
The new section for the dead of the current war has been
added to the graves of the soldiers of the Ukrainian People's
Republic and the Ukrainian Galician Army, who fought
during and after the First World War, a memorial to the
unknown soldier of the Waffen SS 'Galicia' Division, a unit
that consisted of Ukrainians but was part of the German

Armed Forces in the Second World War, and the graves of fighters of the Ukrainian nationalist resistance during the same war. In addition, this military pantheon is located in very close proximity to the cemetery of the 'Lwów Eaglets,' the young Polish insurgents of the 1918–1919 battle for Lviv, and a section containing the graves of the Red Army soldiers killed in the Second World War. These armies once fought against one another: the Ukrainians fought the Poles, the Soviets fought the Ukrainians, and on it went.

It brings some comfort to know that these one-time enemies are now reconciled in death, even if they are confined to different sections of the cemetery. Yet if you walk a little farther, you notice one other burial site, where the graves of the fighters of the Polish November Uprising of 1830–1831 are located. It contains memorial plates with an inscription from Virgil's *Aeneid* (this time the original, not a parody): 'Out of my dust, unknown Avenger, rise!' The inscription is over one hundred years old, but its message hasn't lost its power.

'Honorable Burial Section No. 76' was what I had written in my notepad during my chat with Liuba in the airport. The hearse stopped just before we reached that part of the cemetery and the young men in uniform were once again summoned to carry the coffin. Suddenly, as if the whole thing wasn't heart-breaking enough, we heard a Ukrainian folk song coming out of some speakers. I knew the song well: it is about a man who foresees his death in a war and asks his mother not to scold him. The song had played at the burials of the dozens of protesters murdered by the riot police in the Maidan protests of 2013–14. It had played during the ceremonies attended by thousands and watched on television and on the internet by millions, and it had become associated with the recent war casualties too. It had become the unofficial national song of lamentation.

The song finished. We were approaching the grave. My uncle, who had lost his sight many years ago and couldn't see any of this, but whose heart must have been breaking as much as my mother's and my own, started to shout: 'Heroes never die! Heroes never die!' Others picked it up and now the uniformed men were marching to this chant. Over the years of war in the Donbas, this chant became a widespread cry of defiance. I knew my uncle and the people who joined him meant well, but I wanted to scream: 'Stop! He *is* dead! They're about to put him in a grave!' This was the third of the three moments I dreaded most of all.

After they played the national anthem, after firing the salute somewhere further up on a hill (far enough that the riflemen could not be spotted but close enough that the gunfire could be heard), the coffin was lowered and covered with earth. I held on to my mum, trying to support her, but she ended up supporting me.

More photographers, more journalists. One of them came up to me and asked me to speak on camera. I murmured something about it not being a good time. She insisted. I barked at her and told her to leave me alone. The next thing I knew, she was interviewing my mother. Two local politicians approached me and gave me their business cards. They said that given the topic of my research, I might find it useful to stay in touch. I had no idea how on earth my research might be of interest to them, or how they had the nerve to exchange business cards at a graveside. I guess, just like the journalists, they were doing their jobs.

And then, suddenly, it was all over. The young men in uniform were given the order to march off. The other officials disappeared together with the hearse. The grave was attended only by the immediate family. Liuba came to say goodbye and to remind me that we could call her any time. Again, she meant it.

The funeral theater was over, and now the real thing began. One of my aunts started to sing a song that is traditionally sung in Ukraine during Lent, about Mary standing by the cross watching her son die. A beautiful lamentation. My mother finally burst into tears. Properly. She had held herself together when others were around. Now, with only her closest people by her side, she could show her feelings. I started to feel a strange sense of peace. All day I had been troubled by a string of questions: Would my brother have liked this pompous funeral? Did he want a church service? Would he have liked being buried in Honorable Burial Section No. 76? Would he have approved of the military salute? But now I let them go. None of that mattered any more. This was the end.

I didn't want to leave the grave, but it was time to go to the wake, to Enei, the convenient restaurant nearby named after the lovable rogue. To sit down and remember my brother's life with people who knew him the way he really was.

The next day, we would get up, drink our coffee, and visit the grave. After that, I would open my notepad and review the tasks that still needed to be done.

13 Twenty-Five Folders

How many pages can twenty-five folders contain? I was musing over this question as my mother and I sat in the office of a regional social security service. We had to visit it the day after the funeral to get some more paperwork sorted out. The death of a soldier turns out to be a much more bureaucratic affair than they show you in the movies. The twenty-five folders I was staring at were large ring binders, similar to the ones I use to keep my teaching materials. They can fit quite a lot of paperwork if you have an efficient filing system. The room we were in was not the most organized of places, but these twenty-five folders brought a sense of order to it. They were carefully labeled:

Maidan Protests (one folder).
Power of Attorney (one folder).
War Casualties (one folder).
Family Members of War Casualties (one folder).
War Veterans (twenty-one folders).

My mother's surname, the same as my surname, typed up and printed, was stored in one of those folders, and her maiden name, the same as my brother's surname, was stored in another. Many other names I knew were scattered throughout these binders. I knew some of them intimately: they were the same as the names of my classmates, neighbors, kids I played with when I was growing up. Other names I had encountered in passing—heard them in news stories, read them online, or on gravestones. Now they were categorized, sorted and filed to make our lives neater, to tidy up our thoughts, to give us a sense of order.

There were lots of women filing things in that room. Their desks overflowed with paperwork. They had to file it away. It felt as though, if they didn't file it, it would take over the whole room, flood the corridor where people were waiting with more paperwork, pour out of the building and onto the streets. It could take over the entire city if it wasn't filed. It was better off in folders where it belonged. Names wandering the streets could be dangerous, they could go places they were not supposed to go: the offices of high officials, the desks of journalists, school textbooks. They could continue to live on individually, waking us up in the middle of the night and reminding us of their existence, of the life they could have had if they hadn't been stored in the files. Or they could join forces and appear in numbers growing day after day and press on us with their mounting strength. Names typed up and filed away lived on too, but their lives were quiet, ordered.

I stared at the twenty-five folders while my mother and I waited for the busy women to call out our names: her surname, the same as my surname, or her maiden name, the same as my brother's surname. Names that were already stored in the folders, printed and filed, making two of the folders slightly thicker, heavier.

'Khromeychuk?' I heard a stern woman's voice. 'Are you here about Pavliv's case?'

'Yes,' my mother said faintly.

'Listen, Missus, are you Khromeychuk or are you Pavliv?'

'Khromeychuk. Pavliv,' my mother replied, confused.

'Well, you need to make up your mind, don't you? We don't have all day here, do we? How many names can one woman have?'

I noticed that my mother looked like a child who had just been told off and was about to apologize for something she hadn't done. I didn't recognize her as the strong super-woman I knew my mother to be. She had barely cried during those hellish days, she had supported me and the rest of the family, she had only occasionally and quietly howled like an injured animal in the middle of the night. And suddenly, the woman in the office with twenty-five folders was about to reduce her to tears. I was having none of it.

'Do you know why we are here?' I asked.

'Yes,' she snapped back angrily, but then somewhat surprised by my presence at her desk.

Most people who come to these offices sit quietly and put up with the rudeness of the staff because they don't want to be sent away empty-handed and told to come back tomorrow, or the day after tomorrow, or next month.

'I can see that you are married. Did you change your name when you got married? Most women did in the USSR?' I asked and saw a look of shock on her face.

How dare I ask her about her personal life? It is she who deals with other people's problems; her own life is nobody's business!

'Yes,' she said, more quietly than the first time, probably out of surprise rather than politeness.

'So, what is your problem with my mother's name? She also had it changed when she got married.'

My question didn't solicit a verbal response, but the answer came in the change of attitude.

'Have you got the paperwork for us?' she asked calmly.

I pulled out the newly acquired death certificate, a copy of my brother's passport and my brother's military papers, and handed them over to her. She asked us to wait again.

As we waited, I inspected the rest of the office: the place was filled with shabby seats in the waiting area, there was only one working computer for the entire team of people, and only one toilet for the entire floor — it didn't need signposting because you could find it using your sense of smell. I understood why the woman was cross with my mother: she saw her as someone who was privileged, because she came from abroad. She didn't know my mother's circumstances, what sort of life she had abroad, but, surely, anything must be better than working in this office, right? That's what she must have thought. That's why in spite of knowing the reason for our being there, she sank into habitual rudeness. Noticing my anger, my mother held my hand and told me to calm down, told me it wasn't worth it.

We sat there watching the woman photocopy the papers we had given her and file them away. She approached us again.

'You can go now. Your papers are safe here. We'll look after them.' She spoke to us with what looked like regret in her eyes.

We left the room. We left a bit of ourselves in that room, among those twenty-five folders. And we were grateful to the woman for looking after what we had left behind.

14 Masha

'You only call me 'Maria' when you are cross with me. Are you cross with me?' asks Masha when I use her full name while speaking to her on Skype. I *was* cross with her then. I don't remember why now. Probably because I noticed that she had been too friendly with radical nationalists, and I thought that that was dangerous for her, for her cause, for her reputation. I thought it was wrong. She didn't think it was right either, but she was less naïve or less self-righteous than I was.

It's funny that I normally call her Masha: we are both from western Ukraine, where Maria becomes Marichka, Marusia, but not Masha. Masha is the Russian diminutive and if you use it, it suggests that you are a Russian-speaker, which neither of us is. But that is how she was introduced to me when we first met and that is the name I used when I wasn't cross with her.

I first contacted Masha to interview her in 2014 because I wanted to know about her involvement in the Maidan protests. It was soon after the demonstrations had finished; the protest camp city still stood in the middle of Kyiv, some fires were still smoldering, crosses and other makeshift shrines had started to appear where people had been shot. Central Kyiv looked post-apocalyptic. It looked as if a war had just ended. In fact, the war was just beginning, but we didn't know that on the day we met.

Masha waited for me in a hipstery little café for two hours. I kept texting her that I was running late, and she waited. I had been held up by my previous interviewee, a radical nationalist who turned up very late to the interview smelling of alcohol even though it was ten in the morning. The interview turned out to be pointless and I didn't use it in the article for which I had collected it. The interview with Masha was quite the opposite: I collected enough material to fill a book. But most importantly, I acquired a new friend.

When I finally got to the café, I saw a striking young woman. Tall, with a long, messy ponytail, she looked younger than me, but projected such confidence that I muddled my words as I tried to introduce myself and apologize for my lateness.

'So, you are a British scientist then,' she said sarcastically when I told her I was from the UK. 'British scientists' is a phrase that is much used by the media in Ukraine whenever a new invention is being promoted, and it's often meant as a joke. 'British scientists confirm that this laxative is the most effective cure for constipation.' That's the sort of thing you hear in the endless commercial breaks on Ukrainian TV. Sarcasm did not seem like a good start to an interview. But I really didn't know how to fix things.

She got up and said: 'Let's go outside. I need a smoke.' I followed her obediently. Masha chain-smoked and told me the story of her involvement in the protests. It was only then that I noticed that her deep green eyes were still seeing those images of death and destruction. She looked shell-shocked as she searched for the words that could adequate- ly describe what had just happened to her and her country. Eventually, she forgot that she was speaking to a 'British scientist,' or maybe just warmed up to me, and relayed her experiences of the Maidan the way they had etched them- selves in her mind. This was her first interview. She didn't realize at the time that she would be asked similar questions again and again by researchers and journalists for years to come.

Masha is well-known in Ukraine now. It is the sort of fame that people gained quickly and unexpectedly when the Maidan had just finished and the war was just starting. Be- tween Viktor Yanukovych fleeing the country and the new presidential elections, activists and volunteers took over the functions of the state and, in many ways, turned out to be more efficient than the government. Volunteers collected everything that the army needed, demanded punishment for those who had shot at civilians during the protests, and many joined the army and went to the front.

Masha did everything she could during the protests. She made Molotov cocktails and gave speeches on gender equality. After experiencing discrimination from male pro- testers, she secured permission to talk about equal rights from the Maidan's central stage but had to wait until late in the evening for it to become free. When she was about to be given the microphone, several men (fellow protesters) stopped her and said:

'You know, what I have between my legs, and what you have between your legs are two different things. You should do what you do well: borscht, sewing.'

Masha was having none of that. She went up on the stage and delivered her speech. As it turned out, it was the first of many on the subject of women's rights.

When the war started, she packed up and went to the front. She taught herself to fly drones and then set up an organization that taught others to fly them. She argued that in the 21st century we should not be fighting with people, we should use technology. And it's not as if the Ukrainian Army lacked technology. Volunteer organizations like Masha's, the Ukrainian diaspora and Western governments provided a steady supply of drones for the army, but a combination of untrained soldiers, overly cautious officers and corrupt generals meant that in the early years of the war, some of these drones either never made it to the frontline or ended up in storage somewhere to make sure that they didn't get broken. As Masha pointed out, some officers in charge were worried about being told off by superiors for damaging army property. It seems that damaging people was less of a concern.

Masha wanted to change all this. She organized free training courses for others and flew drones herself at the front. She enjoyed the best of both worlds: she went to the frontline every few months and felt like she was making a meaningful contribution to the war effort, but she didn't sign an official contract with the army and thus couldn't be totally controlled by it. The state also benefited from this situation: it had someone who provided free training, drones, and risked her own life at the front, and if something happened to her, the state bore no responsibility. In her flat, on her desk, there was a pile of requests from various army units asking her to train their personnel — for free, of course.

I admired her determination. But I also realized that the more Masha and people like her did the job of defending the country, something that should have been done by the professional military, the more the state would feel that it needed to do nothing. When I reproached her for enabling the state to assume a passive role while volunteers did the hard work, she asked me how her stopping flying drones or training others would help the people on the frontline. When I told her to be careful with her friendships with radical nationalists, because, after all, they tend to see feminists as a threat to national security and are the most ardent supporters of patriarchy and gender discrimination, things she so passionately tried to fight against, she replied that there were only two categories of people on the frontline: decent people and assholes. Nationalists could be found in both camps; she tried not to hang out with the assholes. When I tried to persuade Masha to take a break from saving Ukraine and look after her health, she smiled in response and said she would. I wasn't convinced by any of these answers.

In her attempt to help those on the frontline, she tried to have the laws on army recruitment changed in order to stop (or at least minimize) discrimination against women. When Masha first started to go to the warzone, she noticed that women were doing everything from kitchen duties to taking part in combat and were often responsible for both at the same time. Because of restrictions in the recruitment law, the majority of army positions—and not only combat ones—were inaccessible to women. As a result, female snipers were registered as administrators and female combat fighters as seamstresses. The state, again, was happy to use people's willingness to risk their lives at no cost to its budget.

These women were completely unprotected when it came to frontline injuries: how do you explain a firearm wound received by an administrator? They were not remunerated adequately, because you don't pay a seamstress additional money for participating in combat. The status they enjoyed was nowhere near that of their male colleagues. Indeed, if things went very wrong and a servicewoman with a semi-legal status was killed, her family would get no compensation. The woman could be blamed for going to the frontline of her own choice; she should have known that it's 'no place for a woman'. And, of course, women were vulnerable to frequent sexual harassment and violence from their own men, not to mention the enemy if they were unlucky enough to be captured.

Masha wanted to change all this too. Like flying drones, she thought she could do it from within the army. I told her that you couldn't reform such a patriarchal institution from the inside, because you would only legitimize it by joining it. She disagreed. We had many heated discussions after which I sometimes thought that she would never speak to me again. At other times she found my arguments persuasive. Despite my skepticism, she persevered: she lobbied the Ministry of Defense, encouraged women veterans and servicewomen to demand their rights, and became an outspoken critic of the military as an institution while supporting the frontline daily. And her efforts paid off. The discriminatory laws were altered as a result of the campaign she had started and led. She did not achieve gender equality in the army, but she took the vital first step towards it. More importantly, at least in part thanks to the advocacy campaign initiated by Masha and women like her, servicewomen started to be regarded not primarily through the lens of their gender, but as professionals who made a choice to join the army.

When I called Masha to say that my brother had been killed, she happened to be at the front. She said that she'd go to the unit where he had served to pick up his stuff and bring it to us. On her way back from Luhansk *oblast*, her car broke down. A walking stick in one hand—she was suffering from an injured leg—my brother's belongings in the other, she boarded train after train and eventually made it to Kyiv. A few days later, when I arrived in Kyiv, we sat in her little kitchen in an old Soviet-style apartment and went through my brother's things together. There, on her kitchen floor, lay my brother's life of the past two years, and we had to work our way through it piece by piece.

After the funeral and a week of bureaucratic hell I thought the worst was over, but I was wrong. Masha, my mother, my partner and I went through everything carefully, sorting it into three piles: stuff that could be useful to others (uniform, boots, backpack, etc.), stuff that could be thrown away (which wasn't much, because one doesn't accumulate much clutter at the front), and stuff we wanted to keep. I took his phone, documents and a khaki scarf; my mother kept the helmet liner with the hole in it, the one he must have been wearing when the shrapnel pierced it; and we kept a t-shirt for my other brother. That was it. The useful pile was quite sizable, and Masha was tasked with finding a volunteer who could pick it up and make sure that it was given to those who needed it. She did this in minutes. I saw the experience acquired through her front-line volunteering in action. She dialed a couple of numbers and in a business-like tone said:

'I've got the family of a fighter here. He was killed in action. His relatives want to make sure that his things can serve others. Can you arrange it?'

Someone came to her flat almost straight away. This was such a relief: we didn't have to transport my brother's belongings somewhere or pack them up and take them with us, not knowing what to do with them other than go through them later and weep again. Masha dealt with it all quickly and efficiently. We were grateful.

Another time I saw her war experience in action was when she called my brother's commander, whom she knew from her volunteering. A business-like tone again:

'Hello. I've got one of your fallen fighters' families here. Can you tell me how he died? Okay, I'm putting you on speaker.'

I would never have found that number myself and, if I had, I wouldn't have had the courage to dial it. I wouldn't have thought that the commander had any obligation to tell me what had happened in the warzone. Nor would I want to traumatize him by making him tell me the details. But the phone call she initiated was very helpful — because we did want to know how he had died, even if we didn't want to ask. As with the belongings, she allowed us to take a back seat while she sorted out the rest. We were grateful again.

As it turned out, my brother's last job was to stand in a trench to determine where the enemy shelling was coming from and pass the information on to those who could return fire. He managed to pass on the details of three attacks. The fourth one killed him. This was no job for a human being. This was a job for a drone. Perhaps one of those sitting in storage not being damaged. Perhaps one of those Masha could have trained another soldier to use. My brother, perhaps.

Masha and I met as researcher and respondent. But we became friends, because only a friend can bring your brother's things from the frontline, help you go through them on her kitchen floor, and find out the facts of his death. We try to stay in touch even if the time difference and our busy lives make it difficult. We argue about many things, but in the end, I still almost always call her Masha.

15   A Pair of Boots, Part II

The bag lying on Masha's kitchen floor in Kyiv was the same one I had packed on my own kitchen floor nearly two years earlier in London. I didn't recognize many items: the uniform was not the British Army one I had bought. It was made of thin, plastic-like material. Some of the t-shirts were the ones from my shopping list, but they no longer smelled of the warehouse as they had when I got them in the post. Now they smelled of earth and damp. The helmet liner was there. The same one I had bought. Except now it had a hole and several brownish stains on it. Some of the leather crosses were still there. Perhaps he didn't offer them to his friends, or maybe they felt that if the bullet-proof jackets couldn't protect them, nothing could. There were some condoms in a small pocket. I hadn't thought of those when I was packing the bag all those months ago.

There was a mobile phone. It had no lock, no password. I didn't know if I should open the text messages, pictures and videos. They didn't belong to me, yet I also felt that they could tell me something. I really needed clues about his life at the front. I wanted to see if he had kept the messages I had sent him. But I knew he wouldn't have liked it if I checked his phone without his permission when he was alive. Why should I not require permission now that he's dead? Eventually, I decided to take a quick look at the phone. The temptation was too strong to resist. I picked it up from the kitchen worktop where it had been charging and noticed that the phone was now asking me for a password. I couldn't understand how that had happened. Only an hour or so earlier when I had turned it on no password was required. There was something a little spooky about this. I put the phone down again and turned it off.

Sometime later, however, my curiosity got the better of me and I turned the phone back on. No password was required again! Really? As I was thinking about what to do, the request for the password reappeared. Now, that was too much for my tired brain. I had a glass of water and decided that when things get too uncanny the only way to deal with them is with the help of reason. I turned the phone off and on again and as expected, for the first few minutes, it didn't ask for a password. That was my window of opportunity: the first few minutes before the password protection program kicked in. I was still uncomfortable about reading his texts and viewing his pictures. So, I put the phone to the side and decided I would take a proper look at it later.

There was also a folder with some paperwork: a brief handwritten autobiography, some military documents, vouchers for free train journeys for soldiers (most of them unused), a list of the next of kin, some pictures of the sun and rainbows drawn by school kids for soldiers. And there was a book with pages missing. A weird fantasy book. I guess weird fantasy is what one needs when weird reality gets too much.

And then I saw them: the Gore-Tex Pro Combat British Army boots. Size 8. They were still in very good shape, although not brand-new anymore. I guess now you would qualify them as 'pre-owned'. They were covered in mud. The fertile, sticky Ukrainian black earth.

I took them into the hall of Masha's flat. The hall was covered in other people's shoes: some were cleaner, newer and more colorful than others. The pair I held in my lap stood sharply apart from the rest. There, among the civilian shoes, this army gear looked like it came from another planet. I cried for the first time since I received the bag. My tears started to roll down my cheeks and onto the shoes. I took a cloth and started to clean them. Gently, like I had at home after I had received them in the post. First, I removed the mud from the soles, then cleaned the rest of each shoe, and gave them a shine. I stroked them, like I had two years ago, and whispered to them: 'Good luck! You can keep someone else dry and warm now.'

16 Volodya, Part II

While going through my brother's things in Masha's flat, we found two thick, white envelopes secured with a white ribbon. The thicker one said '19,500' on it, and the thinner one said '6,790'. I didn't open them, but I realized that they contained money: Ukrainian hryvnias, around £600 and £200 respectively. The thicker one belonged to my brother: he was due to go on leave a few days after he was killed and must have taken most of his money out of the bank in anticipation. The other sum was collected by his comrades for his family, for us, after he was killed.

We had already sorted the rest of his belongings and agreed that most of them should be donated to volunteers who would know what to do with them. My mother and I, without even consulting one another about it, asked Masha to find a volunteer who would take the envelopes too. We were grateful to my brother's comrades for collecting money for us, but we had not spent anything on the funeral (apart from the wake), as everything had been paid for by the state, so it only made sense to pass the money on to help others affected by the war. The same went for my brother's envelope, the contents of which he would never spend on leave.

'Hi! Do you have anyone in acute need now? Right. Medication? Which hospital? Okay, we'll be there soon.'

Masha put the phone down. As always, the efficiency of the volunteers was impressive. It turned out that there was a young man who was in need of long-term medical care but could not access any state support. He had fallen between the cracks in the system: he had volunteered to fight at the front, and then just before transferring to a regular army unit he sustained a terrible injury. He lost half of his stomach, his limbs were badly wounded, and his life was left hanging by a thread. At the time of his injury, he had not been officially recruited by the army and, thus, was not their responsibility. He had been going from one hospital to another for 18 months, completely dependent on the help of the volunteers. One of these volunteers said that he definitely needed some money to buy medication. We jumped into a taxi and headed to the hospital.

As we walked through the long, cold hospital corridors, I breathed in the smell of medicine that I so hated since childhood and tried not to get a migraine from the unpleasantly bright blue-green paint on the walls.

Just before we entered the ward, we were warned by the volunteer:

'You know, he might be in a bad mood. He will most probably not want to accept your help. He can be a bit difficult, which is understandable, of course. He has no one. Well, he has a family, but I don't think they are in touch.'

'What is his name?' my mother asked.

'Volodya.'

We both fell silent.

'How old is he?'

'Forty-two.'

I didn't know if I could enter the ward. I didn't know if I could handle encountering a man of my brother's age with my brother's name who was badly wounded, in a terrible state, with only volunteers to help him, but who was alive when my brother was dead. I didn't know if I would feel pity, resentment, or something else altogether. Most importantly, I didn't want to see my brother in him. I was scared that both my mother and I would want to take care of him the way we couldn't take care of my brother, to 'adopt' this Volodya as some sort of penance for losing ours.

We entered the ward. The stench of medication and cleaning products only worsened. Eight beds in one room. I had only seen such things in black-and-white films about the Second World War where they showed you heroes of the Soviet Union convalescing after their battles. The only difference was that this ward was in color and had a small TV in the corner which everyone seemed to be ignoring. This ward hadn't been conjured into being by a Soviet film director. It was very real. Some men were walking around. One was standing by the window. Volodya couldn't walk or stand. He was lying in his bed. He was expecting us.

I don't know if it was my grieving mind playing tricks on me, or whether this Volodya really did look a bit like my brother. He had a thin, handsome face and long, light-brown hair. He had deeply sad eyes which sparked with anger now and again. My instinct was to sit next to his bed, take his hand, try to soothe him and say that it was okay to be angry at the stinking hospital, the stupid TV in the corner, at us, who had come here uninvited, offering help he hadn't asked for. At the war, the mine that had ripped his stomach open, at himself, at the world.

Instead, I stood next to the door, nodded to say hello, and let my mother sit near him and do the talking. She too seemed unsure of how to behave. She knew her own son wasn't keen on listening to her most of the time so why would this stranger wish to listen to her now? We tried not to cry. We tried not to say anything that could upset him. There were long silences between short sentences. I tried not to look him in the eye. I was scared that he would understand that I was looking for my brother in him. I didn't want him to think that he was a 'substitute Volodya' to us.

Of course, he didn't want to accept the envelopes, but when we said that we didn't know what to do with them either and that he would be doing us a favor by taking them and making use of them, he seemed to give in. He said he'd share the contents with others who were in need.

We left the ward and the hospital. I had never been happier to inhale fresh air. The stuffiness of the hospital and the hopelessness of the ward had been suffocating and made me feel dizzy. I wanted to leave as quickly as possible. I felt guilty for being so lucky, so privileged, so healthy. I felt bitter that there were people who could visit their brothers in hospitals, whereas I had to visit mine in the cemetery. I wanted to stay in touch with the volunteer to ask how Volodya was getting on, but I forgot to take her contact details. I wanted to forget all about *this* Volodya for fear of using care for him to replace grief for *my* Volodya, but in the end I knew that I would always remember him.

17 Mama

'My back was really sore. The midwife was rubbing it to ease the pain and asked me: "Do you want a boy or a girl?" We didn't have any ways of telling a baby's gender in those days. I said: "A boy." She looked at me, surprised. I said: "Girls' lives are so much harder." How wrong I was.'

My mother wasn't wrong. She gave birth to a baby boy when she was barely out of her teenage years herself. His life didn't turn out to be easy, but it wasn't as hard as hers. Suffice it to say, few things can be harder than burying your own child, your firstborn.

I like to ask her sometimes what it was like before my other brother and I came along, when it was just her and him. This woman that so often looks to me like she is made of iron tells me stories that melt my heart. Perhaps, when she was twenty-one and he was a baby, she wasn't made of iron. Or maybe that iron core was always there — otherwise she would have broken long ago. The subsequent years simply tempered the metal base and made what was inside, what kept her together through all that hardship, show a little on the outside. But when she remembers my brother's birth, the early years of his life, the armor that she grew to defend herself against everything that life threw her way falls away. Her face lights up, her eyes fill up with warmth, her voice softens.

'I loved holding him next to my face. So close that I could feel his skin against my cheek. So near that I could smell his hair. I wanted to hear him breathe. I looked at him and couldn't believe that he was real. I couldn't believe that he was mine.' She lifts her tired wrinkly fingers to her face to show how close she held the baby. Her face beams with a smile, so unusual. She can see that child from her youth so clearly that I can almost see him too, reflected in her eyes.

I ask her why she thinks she loved him so. She says she doesn't know. I feel like I need to provide an answer to fill the awkward silence, so I make a suggestion: 'Perhaps it's because you finally had something, I mean someone, of your own. You'd never had anything that belonged only to you before he came along.' As soon as it comes out of my mouth, I feel stupid. I had added difficult memories to memories that seemed so sweet, so precious. She says: 'Perhaps.' I haven't ruined the magic entirely. She is still looking somewhere beyond me. She can still feel the soft skin against her cheek, albeit in memory; a memory that is forty-five years old today.

This is the third birthday that we must celebrate without the birthday boy, already two and a half years after his death. When he was alive, we didn't meet up on his birthday. We all lived far away from each other. We would maybe text one another asking if Volodya had been in touch, if he'd returned anyone's texts. On one birthday after he joined the army I was the lucky one who got through to him on the phone. We had a really nice chat. I put the phone down and called my other brother immediately, urging him to call Volodya, because he had reception on his phone, he hadn't had a drink and he was in a chatty mood. This presented a rare chance to have a conversation uninterrupted by the failure of technology or by inner demons. Yura did as I suggested. We were both pleased. We managed to talk to our eldest sibling, and, for once, it felt like a real birthday.

After Volodya's death, his birthdays became a reason for us to meet as a family. To sit and remember together. To try and focus on good things, funny things. To bring up difficult memories carefully. Once, my other brother remembered that, when he was little, one of the General Secretaries died in the USSR (he couldn't remember which one; there was a period when they were dying one after another) and *Swan Lake* was playing on the TV on a loop. Whenever there was an emergency in the Soviet Union, for some reason they used to put *Swan Lake* on the TV to fill the airwaves. The flags were lowered in the streets, everyone was in a somber mood and Yura was crying because he thought that a war was about to start. This, in a Soviet kid's head, naturally meant that the Germans were going to come and kill everyone. He remembered Volodya calming him and saying: 'Don't worry, we'll go to the countryside, dig a trench and fight them off.' Yura almost got it right: the war started a few decades later, only it wasn't against the Germans.

I talked about my memory of when both of my brothers teased me about St Nicholas. St Nicholas is my favorite saint because, in Ukraine, on 19th December, in the middle of the night, he brings presents and puts them under your pillow while you are asleep. He comes with an angel and a devil, and if you've not been a good child, the devil leaves a stick for you. I always got a stick, a very small, unthreatening one. But I also got a lot of presents. The most exciting part was when the three of us would sit and wait for St Nicholas's arrival. We pledged not to fall asleep or to wake each other if one of us did. The outcome was always the same: I would wake up in the morning, and hear my brothers excitingly sharing stories about seeing big-bearded St Nicholas, the beautiful angel and the scary devil. They would tell me that I had fallen asleep just before they all arrived, and they didn't want to wake me in case I scared away the magical guests. I would cry inconsolably because I had missed the scene I so longed to see, and because they hadn't woken me up, which amounted to a total betrayal. It was only the thought of presents unfailingly waiting under my pillow that would eventually cheer me up.

My father's turn to share a memory came. He said he couldn't think of anything. After an awkward silence he said: 'All I can remember is this time when I picked him up from the kindergarten. He kept chatting, telling stories. He was so excited.' Now, that was a revelation. I never realized that my brother had been a chatty kid, especially with my dad. 'Are you sure you are talking about Volodya?' I asked to make sure he wasn't confusing him with my other brother. 'Yes,' came the brief and confident answer. I felt that there was more to that memory, but I didn't want to push. We all reminisced voluntarily. Our new tradition of celebrating Volodya's birthday was still very fragile. It had to be handled with care.

The most vivid memories are those that my mother keeps, and I like to listen to them when no one else is around. So, the two of us try to meet before the rest arrive; I pour us some coffee and she pours her heart out. She too has a kindergarten story to share. I had heard it before, when Volodya was alive, but hearing it now is a different experience.

'I will never forget when I came to pick him up from the kindergarten wearing a new dress. I didn't have many dresses and rarely bought something new. So, he immediately spotted that I looked different. He was little and rather than commenting on my dress he simply said: "Mama is so beautiful, so beautiful!" I remember it as if it happened yesterday.'

'He was always waiting for me to pick him up from the kindergarten. And later, I was always waiting for him to come home from somewhere. In the 1990s, when he was a teenager, he was really into horse riding. I waited for him at the tram stop after his training to make sure he got home safely. In those days, you didn't need much to get into trouble. Older boys could approach you and ask for a cigarette. If you didn't have one, you could get beaten up. If you had one, you could still get beaten up. I worried and waited.'

I have my own memories of those turbulent days. Once, a boy only a little older than my brother was stabbed in our neighborhood. My brothers knew him well. I was so scared for both of them that I had nightmares of someone chasing them with an axe almost every night for about a year. My mother continues her story...

'That night I waited and waited. The trams came and went but he was nowhere to be seen. There were no mobile phones in those days, and we didn't even have a landline then. I couldn't call anyone to see if he was okay. I must have gone through all the worst scenarios in my head. Suddenly, he came out of a tram. I was so happy. I said: "Volodya, where the hell were you?" He said: "Mama, one of our guys fell off his horse and we had to walk him home to make sure he was alright." At first, I was quite cross that he hadn't found a way to tell me he was going to be delayed, but my anger passed quickly. I remembered when I had fallen off a horse as a young girl and broken my arm. I stopped telling him off.'

My mother was happy that her son was safe. She was proud that he had been busy looking after his friend.

My mother pauses before continuing her memories. We drink our coffee. As she follows her son's life, my mother's memories grow heavier with pain.

'I didn't mean to be a bad mother. But I was so inexperienced. When Volodya went on a school trip, I prepared everything for him as best I could, but when he came back, he was so upset. He said: "I felt so ashamed when all the kids got their flasks out and I had my tea in a bottle where it had already gone cold!" How could I have known about these flasks? We never had a thermos flask in our house. I hadn't heard of one until he told me about it. I felt so embarrassed about my ignorance.'

As she was beating herself up, I thought about how cruel children could be. I thought how sad it was that a woman who had done everything she could for her children, could be so convinced that she had been a bad mother to them because of a stupid flask.

I ask her about the birthday party she arranged for Volodya when he turned eighteen. It was in a restaurant with lots of guests. I must have been nine years old, but my memory of it is very hazy. All I remember is mum and dad running around trying to organize everything, cakes being delivered to the flat and taken straight to the restaurant, and my brother looking all grown up in his smart, brand-new jacket. I still have a photo of him in that jacket. He looks like a kid who wants to be taken for an adult. My mother doesn't have many memories to share from that party. Maybe she only remembers the things she 'didn't get right'.

There was always a special bond between my eldest brother and my mother. Their love–hate relationship was so powerful. They could say the most painful things to each other, but it was her he called in the middle of the night before a battle to ask her to pray for him. She always prayed for him anyway. She didn't need to be reminded.

The last time our family got together was in the chapel at the morgue before my brother's funeral. The priest had finished the service and left. We had the whole evening to ourselves. I was in hysterics. My other brother looked like he was in denial. We stood on either side of the coffin. My mother stood in the center, directly facing my brother's body. She talked to him as if he was still there, as if he could hear her, but just wasn't responding. Much as it often was when he was still alive. His lack of response and our unwillingness to interrupt her monologue allowed her to say everything that lay heavy on her chest. She kept talking, arguing, apologizing, and arguing again. Eventually, she ran out of things to say or simply tired of speaking when there was no reaction to her words. Still directing her words at my brother's motionless face, she said: 'Look at you now! We're all here, we've come to you from far away! And you're just lying there. Like a prince!' Her words were so out of place that we all burst out laughing.

The next day, before they closed the coffin, my mother touched my brother's arms and legs as if to check that he was warm, comfortable. The way you touch your children when you put them to sleep.

When she was twenty-one, she wanted a boy because she suspected that girls' lives were harder. Now in her 60s, she knew it for a fact.

17 Harvest

To every thing there is a season, and a time to every purpose under the heaven.
Ecclesiastes 3:1

'Mama,' cried a man as he fell down.

'Mama,' whispered another as he looked up at the sky for the last time.

'Mama,' thought a woman as she struggled to breathe and watched her plaited blonde hair turn red with a sticky fluid.

'Mama,' and then silence forever.

The noise of war can be very loud. It drowns everything else out. No one heard their last words. Not even Mama.

'A time to be born, and a time to die.'

My hands shaking, I opened the folder that contained the photos on your phone. I didn't know whether you had taken them or whether they had been sent to you. There were pictures of the landscapes of eastern Ukraine, the beautiful steppe I've never had the pleasure of seeing with my own eyes. Weeping willows reflected in a lake. A boat resting by the lake's shore. Coffee brewed on a makeshift fire. Venus shining brightly at night. A lonely cloud against the blue sky. An explosion on an otherwise enchanting horizon. A piece of shrapnel on a path. An empty trench. And photos of this.

An open mouth. An awkward pose, prostrated on the ground. One leg twisted unnaturally to the side. Another in the position of a runner at full speed. Both arms above the head, as if waving to signal: 'I am here! Don't leave me! Take me with you, alive or dead, but don't leave me on my own! Not here. Not forever.'

In the tranquil fields, near the lake: fruit is born out of war.
This region is very fertile. Whatever you plant in the black earth is
accepted graciously and then, the following year, the lush soil
produces a plentiful harvest.

'A time to plant, and a time to pluck up that which is
planted.'

Let's take a closer look. It's not a pretty sight and not some-
thing people want to witness, although, sooner or later, it happens
to us all. It just takes a different amount of time for different peo-
ple. For instance, a corpse that is left in the open air decomposes
four times faster than one that is buried in the ground. But what
has just died very quickly comes to life. Perhaps it doesn't even die
at all. Perhaps one form of life simply transforms into another.

Moments after death, as soon as the process of decomposition
starts, a whole ecosystem appears and flourishes. What happens is
a sort of self-digestion. When the heartbeat stops, and there's no
more oxygen in the cells, they start to break down. This process
starts in the liver, continues in the brain, and eventually takes
hold of all the tissues and organs. The temperature in a corpse
comes to match that of its environment. As rigidity envelops the
body from the face down through the neck, into the limbs, deprived
of energy, the corpse is locked motionless.

And that is when a new type of life begins. The immune sys-
tem stops working, and the bacteria get down to business. They
start to consume the body inside out, digesting the intestines, the
tissues, the capillaries, moving on to the liver, the heart and the
brain. What is not self-digested becomes a feast for creatures with
an acquired taste. Some insects spend their whole life cycle in a
dead body. And what is not consumed by maggots, blowflies, ants,

and beetles is eaten by scavengers. Unlike squeamish humans, they don't mind the odor of rotting flesh. In fact, they are drawn to it.

'A time to break down, and a time to build up.'

There, in the tall grass, barely visible because the khaki colors still camouflage it well, lies a fruit of this war. Unlike the body that disintegrates into the environment around it, our outer, material layer can survive much longer. The boots are completely intact with the shoelaces tied as they were when they had been put on. The trousers are a little worn out because of the rain and the vegetation that grows around them. The belt is done up, its buckle is still shiny, its leather is still firm, unlike the human skin that only just clings to the ribcage that sticks out above it. The ribs are held together with the remnants of a green-brown t-shirt. The t-shirt bears the imprint of a skeleton on it, much like those that children wear at Halloween as they go trick-or-treating.

'A time to search and a time to count as lost.'

At the side, where the heart once was, there is a huge hole in the t-shirt and in the ribcage. It allows us to see the spine. The vertebrae are held together by a mixture of bodily matter, tree leaves and earth. The spine looks like a sculpture ready for display in a museum of modern art. Just above the neckline, there are beads of white. A rosary that must have been worn to deliver its owner from evil. It is still there. Undamaged. Unlike organic matter, plastic doesn't decompose. The mouth is wide open, as if to say 'ah', when a doctor examines your sore throat. Or maybe 'mama'. The teeth are white and strong. Only a couple of gold crowns shine, so out of place in this still life of brown and green, pale ivory and black.

'A time to kill, and a time to heal.'

It is strange to see a skull where there should have been a face. There are only gaping holes where the eyes once were. This body is near the end of the death cycle. The rotting leaves and the wilting grass around it are the only reminders of life. And even those are fading into stillness. What was once a living being is now becoming part of the landscape.

'A time of war, and a time of peace.'

Such fruits of war are scattered all around this bountiful land. The earth will gather its harvest if humans don't. It will transfer the energy that was only briefly trapped in the heart and the limbs and breathe it in to release it again and again.

'All go unto one place; all are of the dust, and all turn to dust again.'

19 That Short Story Was So Hard to Write

One of the main reasons I don't like talking about 'what happened', as I still sometimes refer to it, is because of people's reactions to my words. Or, rather, because they feel that they have to react somehow, but they have no idea how. It makes all of us feel awkward: me for bringing up a difficult subject and them for having to respond to it.

There are different types of reactions when you tell someone your brother was killed in a war. I divide them into three categories: instinctive, intellectual and indifferent. Instinctive reactions can include anything from bursting into tears and offering genuine sympathy, to outrage and shock. Intellectuals usually try to offer some sort of commentary or counsel. They try to make you feel better in a constructive way. The indifferent types are the ones who just say: 'Ah, I see.' It's probably because they don't know what to say, so they don't say anything at all. All three reactions are absolutely fine with me. There is only one, a fourth type, that isn't. It is in a category of its own. And it makes me regret talking about what happened.

Once, when I was speaking at a conference dedicated to the war in the Donbas, a young man, a writer, was telling me how he was suffering from writer's block because the war had affected him personally so much that he simply couldn't write.

'I simply can't write,' he said.

I sympathized, because of 'what happened', although I didn't want to tell this young man, whom I barely knew, about it. Later, I heard him read some of his recent short stories in which people, whom he described as his friends, 'fell on the fields of glory,' as he put it. Losing his friends was very sad, of course. I sympathized again, although the stories were full of pathos and did not resonate with my own feelings about the war.

I asked the young writer how he found the courage, the strength, the words for his writing, given that he knew these people personally.

'You wouldn't understand,' he said, 'you don't know what it feels like to be so intimately involved in this war. It is hard to lose your friends.'

I agreed. I asked if he had known them well. It turned out he hadn't. Much of the information about them was from the papers. Ah, the papers! One can certainly learn a lot from them, as my own experience had shown, but much of it has little to do with reality. I didn't say this to the young man, however. So, he continued:

'You see, you are far away, you are abroad, you don't know what it's like to be in the middle of it.'

'No, I don't, and nor do you, because although you are not abroad, you are also far away from the warzone, in the comfort of your home, writing your short stories,' I thought to myself. I didn't say it out loud.

'You can't understand it. It affected me so much. I simply don't know how to cope with all this information, with my feelings. But I don't think you can understand.'

He went on in the same vein for some time.

'Well, actually, I might understand,' I said, stepping out of my comfort zone, where I keep 'what happened' to myself, and decided to share it with the young man.

'I think I can understand what it's like to lose someone.'

'Yes, yes, of course, people lose loved ones all the time, but it's not the same as having one of your friends killed in a war. A young person, in his prime! You can't understand how hard it is to deal with that sort of loss,' he interrupted my hesitant confession.

But I persevered:

'Well, that is actually what I meant. I *do* know how that feels.'

And then I just said it. I told him 'what happened': 'My brother was killed on the frontline. He's buried in the same cemetery as the guy you describe in your short story. Right next to him.'

There. I said it. I could hear myself say it. Like on a stage, for all to hear, not just the young writer. Releasing the words from deep down felt good. It seemed like my chest had opened up and a black crow had flown out of it. It was still near, circling above me, but it was no longer inside me, no longer flapping its wings in a space that was far too small for it. I could hear my words still ringing in my ears:

'My brother was killed on the frontline six months ago. He's buried in the same cemetery as the guy you describe in your short story. Right next to him.'

'Ah, yes, my short story. It was so hard to write it,' continued the young writer, as if he hadn't heard what I had just said.

He continued talking about himself and I immediately regretted telling him about 'what happened'. It felt like we were competing over whose grief was greater. We were both preoccupied only with our own grief, and our own stories, which were so hard to write, to speak, to comprehend. But once the words were out together with the black crow, there was no way of bringing them back in. They had to be poured out one by one.

20 Theater of War

Never before had I been so frightened of looking people in the eye. I couldn't breathe. Why the hell did I start this project? Why did I think it was a good idea? I wanted to cry, to run away, to lock myself in the dressing room and tell everyone that everything was canceled. But it was too late. The deposit for the theater had been paid, we had invested so much time into rehearsals, and, in any case, people had already started to arrive at the small London theater for the first night's performance. They had paid for their tickets. The first two performances were sold out and there was even a long waiting list. All these people had chosen to spend an hour of their precious time watching our show.

I had to pull myself together and face them. My hands trembling, my eyes welling up, my voice breaking, I stood in the entrance to the auditorium watching them come in one by one. When I felt that I was losing my grip I would step into the darkness of the dressing room—all the actors were already on stage—and say a sort of prayer. I wasn't sure who it was addressed to: was I pleading with a divine power to help me do this show well, or begging my brother's forgiveness for using this story in a theater piece and asking him to 'hold my hand' on stage? To help ensure that those who came to see it understood at least some of what I wanted to convey to them. The prayer gave some comfort, and I could step out to greet the audience. Some entered

with a pint of beer or a glass of wine, some with a supportive smile or a hug. They sat down.

The pre-show chatter stopped. The house lights were
still on. I made eye contact with all my actors and the tech-
nician to let them know we were about to start. I stood center stage waiting for my nerves to calm down. I saw my
mother, my father, my brother. All three of them looked
back at me from the audience just as nervously as I was
looking at them from the stage. Deep breath. Okay, I had to
start speaking.

'I don't like talking about what happened. "What happened", that's how I still refer to it most of the time, and I
really don't like talking about it.'

We started the show. The opening line was hard to utter. It had also been the hardest to write. The theater company had agonized over it collectively with me. How does
one start a play about a death on the frontline? You can
whack the audience with the hammer of graphic descrip-
tions of the horrors of war and make them regret that they
booked that ticket right away. You can also be too delicate
and leave them feeling nothing. This was a play about a
brutal war: we didn't want the audience leaving as if nothing had happened. 'I don't like talking about what happened' seemed like a good opening line. More importantly,
it was true.

I hated talking about it and tried not to unless I absolutely had to. My family's lives were permanently split into
a 'before it happened' and an 'after it happened'. 'When did

you speak to so-and-so last?' my mother would ask my brother. 'Oh, it was a while ago. Before, you know, before what happened.' Others around us were using it too. A friend would ask: 'Has your mother been to Ukraine since, you know, since what happened?' A euphemism has its role and power. So, I used it as a gentle opening into the less gentle story of a life lost on the frontline.

People seemed to be listening. The actors were delivering their lines. The scenes changed one after another: the chaos of a social security office turned into a therapy room for a woman suffering from PTSD, a front-line trench turned into a friend's kitchen, then a graveyard, and then back into a theater stage. It was all a blur for me. I regained awareness of reality when the show was over. People came up and gave me a hug. Some were sobbing. I was moved and reassured about the next step — taking the play to the biggest theater festival in the world — the Edinburgh Fringe.

The experience of Edinburgh was sobering. Walking up and down the Royal Mile, the city's busiest street, approaching tourists who wanted to hear jokes about politics was not new to any of us. This was the third show we had brought to the Fringe. But the previous two were comedies, albeit pretty dark. Now we had about five seconds to get each passer-by interested with a flyer and a catchphrase about a war show. I found myself struggling to say to strangers: 'This is a true story. It's about my brother.' My pain was still very private. It was hard enough displaying it in the controlled space of a small theater, never mind on a busy street.

I hadn't thought of this when making the Edinburgh preparations. Nor had I thought of what performing every day for a week, sometimes two shows per day, would do to my mourning process. I just had a compulsion to perform this play for as many people as I could. By the end of the run, I was exhausted and so was the rest of the company. Not only did they work really hard—giving out flyers by day, performing by night—they were also checking up on me, making sure I was okay. By the end of the run, I knew I could go anywhere with them, even into the depths of grief.

And that is where we went next. We decided to keep performing the show in theaters in London but felt that we wanted to develop it further. The major change came when one of the actors had to leave and we needed to replace him. He had been performing the part of my brother. His lines came from the videos that my brother had recorded on the frontline. I found them in Volodya's phone. I don't know who they were made for or why. Perhaps he made them in the hours of desperate loneliness when a phone camera was the only channel through which to converse with the rest of the world. The first one recorded a sunset through a hole in a dugout wall. The second depicted a frozen lake and a snowy landscape. The last one showed the scenery around the trench covered entirely by a thick fog. It ended with a close-up of the sparkling drops of rain on a bare branch. It was recorded just a couple of days before his death.

I had wanted to incorporate the videos into the show but hadn't had the courage to play them on stage. So, I had transcribed and translated the text, and had it delivered by an actor. To give him a soldiery look, I went online once again and bought a uniform and army boots. Facebook, of course, started to advertise all these things to me again, just like the first time. Sometimes I found it amusing and sometimes insufferable. Now that actor had left, and all we had were the uniform and the boots. I decided not to replace the actor but use my brother's actual videos in the show. I seemed to have found the courage to do that now.

The first performance using my brother's videos felt like we were doing it all for the first time again. I had a similar sense of trepidation, but this time not so much because I had to face an audience as because I was about to face my brother, albeit on a screen. The small theater was packed full. We started the show as we had done many times before, but this time, soon after the opening scene, two actors unfurled a sheet of white fabric. I picked up a hand-held projector, knelt down in the middle of the stage so as not to block the screen, selected the first video and played it for all to see. A blood-red sun appeared through piles of earth and my brother's voice narrated the scene:

'Ladies and gentlemen, may I have your attention, please? I present you with the sunrise through a hole in a dugout wall. Of course, you won't be able to see what I see here, it's not the same on the video... See those hills over there?... That's where the enemy is. We are fighting them. See? Anyway, I better take my phone away 'cause they can shoot right fucking at it.'

The video finished, the actors folded the screen, and I could not believe that my brother and I had just met face to face. I wasn't the only one who felt that way. My mother came to see every show, and when people asked her why she did that, she said she came for the encounter with her son. Neither of us could bring ourselves to watch those videos at home anymore, but we did it with a certain joy when they were played on stage.

The inclusion of the videos changed the experience of the show completely for me. Kneeling there, looking at my brother on the screen I sometimes cried and sometimes laughed.

'Hello everyone! This is our position. In the forest. Look how pretty it is. Fuck me! Wiiinteeerr...,' started the second video.

All you could see was dirty white snow all around. Beautiful indeed.

'Down there, there's a village. Over here, there's a lake. Yep, it's a fucking lake alright.'

That phrase and my brother's deadpan delivery always made me giggle. He continued:

'Over there we take cover from all sorts of mines and mortar fire. I really like it when winters are beautiful like this.'

Profound and profane. That's Volodya in a nutshell. And then he hummed a song:

'I ain't got no honey, baby, sugar, baby now...'

I didn't recognize it and had to look it up. It turned out to be an old blues song. The second verse went:

'Who'll rock that cradle, who'll sing that song? / Who'll rock that cradle when I'm gone?'

The line from the recordings that was forever engraved into my memory came at the very end of the last video. After showing his bulletproof vest, radio transmitter, 'communications, optics, and all that shit,' my brother zoomed in on the branches of a bush growing right outside of the trench and said:

'But the most interesting thing here are these drops of rain on the branches. See these droplets? That is the most interesting thing here.'

Two days later he was killed in that very trench. I can only hope that he saw the sparkling droplets against the sky as he waited for the moment of complete peace.

'I'll rock that cradle and I'll sing that song. / I'll rock that cradle when you're gone. / I'll rock that cradle when you're gone.'

[Exit. Curtain.]

21 Ignoble Pain

Grief is full of noble pain. Most people can relate to what you are going through, and when you fall apart there is no shame in it: you lost a loved one, it's understandable. You will not be judged. This sort of pain is ennobling. But that is only what it's like on the surface.

Not long after my brother died, my friend's sister died. She took her own life. I recognized so many of the stages of my friend's grief: the initial shock; the frustration of not being able to accept it, to let it go; the anger at the one who was dead for dying and at yourself for not having done anything to prevent their death; the slow coming to terms with their absence; the desperate attempts to recollect every stray bit of your positive memories; and the emergence of stubborn negative ones. The agony of it all. The guilt. The strange relief that comes from realizing that at least now you don't have to worry about your sibling doing something stupid. They've done it. It's over. The self-loathing that came after such thoughts. The repetition of the cycle of the same feelings over and over again, and the fear that they will never leave you in peace.

Each time I wanted to say, 'I so know how you feel,' but each time I realized that I didn't really know how she felt, because it's one thing to say 'my brother was killed in a war'; it's quite another to say 'My sister took her own life.' It takes guts. The guts my friend had, and I suspected I lacked.

I knew that my outward pain was noble. Some people thought highly of my entire family just because my brother was killed in a war, because that is what any good son of a good family should be prepared to do: 'He gave his life for our peace'; 'He fought for his homeland'; 'He didn't die in vain.' These words were ennobling both for the memory of the dead and for us, the living. Even if I didn't really believe or agree with them, I found that they soothed my grief. But as time went by, the pain that was lurking below the surface became too hard to ignore. And it was far from noble.

At different points in his life, my brother could have died so many other deaths—while working undocumented abroad in dangerous jobs, from pneumonia that wasn't detected on time, on a street while sleeping rough during the most difficult period of his life, in a drunken fight, or in a moment of despair when he slit his wrists. The death that befell him just happened to take place in the circumstances it did: on the battlefield.

Once, when my brother was already serving on the frontline, I was in Kyiv for a conference. We were discussing something related to historical wars, but the war being fought not that far away was on everyone's mind. To mark the end of the conference, the organizers took us all to see a play with a curious title, *My granddad dug, my father dug, but I won't dig*, which was directed by two women—a rare occurrence in the West, let alone in Ukraine—Agnieszka Błońska and Rosa Sarkisian. In the show, one actor kept repeating 'My brother didn't die in war, he died of an overdose.' I didn't know if the line was about the actor's real brother or not, but I thought that the company were very brave to have included it in their piece.

In a country engulfed by war, the value of a human life was rapidly decreasing and the heroic rhetoric about 'our dead' seemed to be the only strategy available to cope with the sorrow stretching across the entire nation and penetrating so many homes. The heroic rhetoric created an illusion that a life lost in war was not a lost life. A life lost to drugs, on the other hand, is often considered a waste. I sat there watching the play and thinking: 'My brother is on the frontline now, only some 500 miles away from this theater, and he could well die there any minute.' My next thought was: 'At least he won't die of an overdose.'

Whether we like it or not, we are socialized to value certain types of death and despise or fear other types. This makes it easier for one sister to say 'my brother was killed on the frontline' and much harder for another to say 'my brother died of an overdose' or 'my sister took her own life'. A sister's grief, however, is not commensurate with societal acceptance of her sibling's death.

A week after watching the play, I got the news that my brother had been killed on the frontline. Was I glad that it wasn't the drugs or the street or losing the will to live that took him away, but a piece of shrapnel in a cold, damp trench? I don't know. I hope not. If I was, I don't think I would fully admit it to myself.

When I started to put my grief into words, I realized that I was selecting the noble bits of my pain and pushing the darkness deeper down. It was there in every line, visible to me, but hidden from others. I let myself delve quite far into my grief but never far enough. Each time I stopped at some invisible fence beyond which the real pain lived. The one that bore no words to describe itself, only the sensation of nausea you experience when you're about to faint. I didn't dare go beyond that fence. I didn't want to faint and lose control. It took me a long time to realize that that nausea was a sign of fear: I was scared of being judged for telling the whole story.

I didn't want to be judged, but more importantly, I didn't want to be afraid of being judged.

My brother died in war—but did this make his death less of a waste? He had a good life. He had a terrible life. He had a life he chose and a life that chose him. His forty-two years were full of adventures, some pursued, some accidental, but all received with what at some points could be called dignity, at others selfishness, and at others still indifference. His fellow soldiers kept repeating that he was a brave man. He didn't need to go to war to prove his courage. It takes guts not to conform and choose freedom over any type of convention, even if this freedom sometimes meant no shelter, food or income. I was determined to be at least half as courageous as he was, and that meant no longer hiding behind my noble pain, and being brave enough to tell the *whole* story.

22 Heart

You were not sure if you were still alive. You couldn't tell whether your heart was still beating, whether your blood was still flowing in your veins. So, you decided to check. You decided to find something sharp that would go right through your skin, your flesh, and split the thin layer covering the pulsating flow inside. You thought: if the red comes gushing through, if it bursts out like a prisoner who's been waiting to be set free for years, if it starts to make the gray and the black around a bit more colorful, you could draw comfort – there was life inside you yet. And when you resolved to keep it that way, you found a cloth to tighten your wound and raised your injured arm above your heart.

I never asked you why you did it. I never asked if you were really so tired of life that you felt ready to see it end. I never asked, but I always wanted to know. So, here's the story I made up to explain it to myself.

You left your former life behind and burned your bridges. You decided that you had had enough. Again. So, you traveled back to the land of your dreams. You passed one city after the next, getting closer and closer to your destination. The place where you could once again be a little boy, loved and protected. The place where you could be a young man who had just fallen in love for the first time. The place you had to leave as an adult, leaving a chunk of your heart there. Or maybe your whole heart. Maybe that is why you hadn't felt your heartbeat for so many years, because it was too far away from the rest of your body. If only you could be reunited with your young heart, you would be whole again. Healed. Alive. That's what you thought.

Crossing the border from your old life to the land of dreams, you had to change trains because the railroad tracks on the other side were different. The wider tracks that start on the eastern edge of Europe serve as a cursed reminder that the iron curtain might be a thing of the past in history books, but its ghost still whispers quietly as you move from one train to the next: 'Are you sure you want to cross the border into the east?' You were sure. You hurried out of the softer, cleaner carriage and moved your few possessions onto the hard, uncomfortable surface of a bunk bed in a train that had seen better days.

The train arrived at its final destination early in the morning. It was at that hour when the night no longer reigns but nor is the day fully in charge. The time when anything is possible, when the trains arrive from afar to give their sleepy travelers the chance to start afresh. The station loudspeakers played a greeting march, a peculiar tradition in the land of dreams. The travelers rolled out of the carriages one by one like balls of wool from an overturned knitting basket; each leaving one end of the thread inside the train, or perhaps even in the station where they had boarded the train, and taking the other end with them wherever they were going, until there would be no more wool left to unroll.

You kicked your bundle of wool off the steps of the train and watched it roll along the platform. The red line ran ahead in a streak, and you followed it. What else could you follow in the absence of your heart? The thread took you out of the station and through the familiar streets. Having passed the new circus and the old theater, the creepy hotel and the cheerful fountain you found *yourself by a familiar building. Something in your chest tightened. You approached the front door, and your fingers pressed the bell. No one answered. The color of the paint on the front door, the smell of the street, the doorbell under your finger. Could they tell you where your heart was?*

The ball of wool led you on. It tumbled around the corner into an old, dilapidated playground. If you closed your eyes, you could have visualized the swings painted bright blue, the sandpit covered with colorful buckets and spades, the benches framed by flowers. If you kept your eyes closed, you could have begun to hear the laughter of the children running around the roundabout: 'faster-faster-faster,' those on the roundabout would have cried with excitement. But you kept your eyes open and didn't see any of that. Instead, you saw some broken wood that might have once surrounded the sandpit, a crooked piece of metal that might have held up the swings. There were cigarette butts lying around the bench, so you took your packet out of your pocket and lit a cigarette. Exhaling the smoke, you could feel your lungs struggling to work and you remembered about your heart.

The red thread took you to a school located in the neighborhood. The large windows still had the same dark frames, the door was still an uninviting brown. The school stood between an infamous prison and the old war-time ghetto. A location that could teach the local children more about the history of this place than any of their teachers would ever dare. You approached the uninviting but familiar door to take a closer look at an unfamiliar plaque near it. It was honoring 'a hero who fell defending his motherland'. You did not recognize the man portrayed on the plaque, but the inscription bore your name. Your name and your date of birth.

Your name, your date of birth and the date of your death. The latter was seven years in the future.

So now you knew that, at least in theory, you had another seven years of life left. The life you couldn't feel. A perfect chance to test that it was in fact there.

You remembered another place you might have left your heart and kicked the wool in that direction. The ball obliged and rolled up a hill, the highest hill in the vicinity. Standing on its peak, you could see the scattered red tiles of the roofs that somehow shaped themselves into a city. As the lights were beginning to appear in the windows beneath the red roofs, you lit another cigarette. Your heart was nowhere to be found. The ball of wool stood still. There was nowhere else to go.

This seemed like the right time and place for your experiment. You looked around to see if any of the revelers who frequented this spot had left anything that could do the job. Much to your surprise, you didn't find any broken glass from empty bottles. But you found a piece of tin. It must have been left over from a snack that had accompanied someone's beer. The piece of tin turned out to be sharp and dived into the arm without any effort. The skin gave way, the flesh began to part, and one red streak trickled down from your arm to join the other lying beside you.

As you watched the red trickle of blood meet the red strand of wool, you realized that you could feel something. The shock of having a feeling was overpowering and prevented you from identifying what this feeling actually was. Joy? Relief? Pain? You felt what could only be described as life. Your experiment had worked! Excited by the thought that there was still life in you, you dropped the arm that held the tin and accidently slashed the thread of wool on its way down.

The city lights started to fade out, as did your cigarette. The feeling of life that had just appeared began to give way to the tightness in the chest you had felt earlier, standing by the familiar building. Eventually, the pressure subsided, and a bird flew out of your chest: a strange creature with red feathers. Flapping its wings as hard as it could, it resembled a beating heart. It landed on the ball of wool lying next to you. The thread you thought you had slashed was still attached to the rest of the bundle, but only just. You tied a knot to secure the connection, used some of the wool to bandage the cut on one arm, and cradled the bird in the other.

The lights of the city were once again glowing before your eyes. You started to think of what you could do with your remaining seven years.

23 Theory and Practice of War, Part II

'This is the last of three sessions we'll have on the Second World War. Before the Easter break — as I'm sure you remember — we looked at the causes of the war and discussed the reasons for the Soviet victory on the Eastern Front. The focus of today's seminar is on the *costs* of the Second World War.'

As I introduced the seminar, I noticed that the students seemed eager to learn; they had rested during the break and were ready to engage in discussion, especially since the exam was imminent and few things can motivate students more powerfully. Nine hours dedicated to the war on the Eastern Front is pretty generous for a history course in a British university. Normally, you would have to rush through everything from causes to consequences in one class and somehow explain the complexity of it all to students. Having three whole hours dedicated to the issue of costs, combined with the enthusiasm of the students, would normally seem like a professional dream come true. Not this year.

Unlike my students, I had returned from the break exhausted, confused and barely able to function in my day-to-day life, not to mention in a professional setting.

Normally, when teaching the class on the costs of war, I would encourage my students to think of the people behind the numbers in their textbooks, because it is individuals who die in wars, ethnic cleansings and genocides; it is actual living, breathing people who become the casualties of wars. These are not abstract losses. Each loss is the loss of a real person, and each individual loss means some family's world being shattered. Now I was trying to imagine what a history book about the war in Ukraine, in which my brother was one of those unfortunate losses, would look like. I tried to perceive him as part of the number of casualties, but I could not. My brother did not fit into any number, no matter how great or small.

'Cost' suddenly seemed like a funny word. I imagined two people having a chat in a market:

'How much are your wars?'

'Oh, it very much depends, sir. Are you thinking of a small local war or a total, world war?'

'A small local one to begin with.'

'Anything between five and twenty thousand.'

'What about a big one?'

'We'll be talking millions, I'm afraid.'

'Millions, eh? I'll stick to the small one for now then.'

'Good choice, sir. Shall I wrap it up for you?'

'No, that's alright. I don't have far to go.'

This grotesque dialogue continued to play out in my head as I was trying to talk to my students about military and civilian casualties, the Shoah, the rapes, the destruction, the traumas.

I spent the rest of the class focusing on the facts and trying to swallow the lump I felt in my throat. I didn't want to share my personal tragedy with my students. I love teaching, it comes naturally to me, but merely performing the role of a lecturer is unnatural. Hiding my true thoughts from my students felt wrong when I asked for an honest and open-minded analysis of history from them. I felt like a failure because I could not distance myself from the subject I was teaching and instead watched neutrality, impartiality, objectivity and all those other qualities that a historian is supposed to possess fly right out of the window. I felt like I would never be able to teach war again. I also started to doubt my ability to research war.

The teaching term ended, but the season of conferences had only just begun. I decided not to cancel any conference commitments following my brother's death. I thought that diving deeper into work about war would help me take my mind off the actual war. I was wrong. Each time I gave a talk, I had a panic attack. I am not sure I realized that they were panic attacks at the time, but I knew that the reaction I had at those conferences was different from the usual nerves one gets before speaking in public. I felt dizzy, breathless, nauseous, a bit like I was going to die. I felt embarrassed and feared that others would see me in that state and think me unprofessional.

I was scared that people would judge my work through the prism of my personal tragedy: 'Her brother died in the war, and that's why she says what she says...' I noticed how the people who knew about my personal connection to the war would glance at me each time someone mentioned 'the families who have lost their loved ones'. I didn't want to be the token soldier's sister. I wanted my professional work to be assessed on its merit. I started to hate conferences and fear the small talk in lunch breaks and evening receptions. The war in the Donbas always came up. I couldn't make small talk about the war.

It was in the middle of one conference, during one specific paper, that I began to understand what sparked such a strong reaction in me. The talk was by a relatively young and relatively reputable academic who spent thirty minutes or so (which was longer than the time allocated to his paper, and which felt like an eternity) theorizing about the ongoing war. The theorizing itself was not upsetting; after all, I was doing something similar myself. Trying to work out the frameworks and language that would allow us to talk about wars is essential. What was upsetting was that while the paper was on the war — that is to say, an event in which people live and die — it was devoid of people entirely. It referred to philosophers and theorists and made smug intellectual jokes. It didn't help that I spotted the author finishing the paper (or even writing it from scratch?) the morning before the talk. It also didn't help that I knew that the honorarium that the speakers received for delivering their papers, me included (something that doesn't happen often, but did at that particular conference) was the same as the monthly salary of those who were serving on the frontline. But all of this would have been fine, I think, if it weren't for what seemed like a disregard for the people the scholar was discussing. I was not expecting sympathy or respect. My own paper was critical of militarization and the culture around heroizing dead soldiers. All I was expecting was some sort of acknowledgment of the subjects as humans, good, bad and ugly, not purely as matter for theoretical analysis and philosophical speculation.

That paper provoked me to have a good think about my own response to the academic work I was doing. Had I become too involved? Had I stopped being a scholar when I became the sister of a fallen soldier? Was I able to be impartial? Should I be impartial? I told myself: it's a job, like any other. You do it, you go home, you forget about it and return to your life. The thing is, my job was never like that even before my brother was killed. It *was* my life, and the discussions of war were my life too. Now that war itself had become part of my life, I desperately wanted it just to become a job, but I didn't know how to do that.

Since my brother's death, the war has been part of my daily existence and I have learned to live with it. I wish I could say that I don't get panic attacks at conferences dedicated to war anymore, but it wouldn't be true. One thing I learned, however, was that personal vulnerability is not a sign of failure; it can be an effective facilitator for a discussion of something so unimaginable and yet so commonplace as war. I've also learned that honesty and impartiality are not incompatible.

'Your classes on the Second World War are different from the other classes I have on the subject,' a student who specialized in War Studies and who was getting ready to join the British army after his degree told me.

'How so?' I asked. He thought for a while, looking for the appropriate word.

'They are *emotional*,' he finally said.

I thought he must have said that because I was one of the very few women in the department who taught war. It was the end of the term and I felt too tired to explain to him why the use of 'emotional' might have been problematic, so I just asked him to clarify what he meant.

'You talk about people. It's all about humans in your classes. Not just battles, but humans,' elaborated the young man.

'Well, it's humans who fight those battles, right? It's humans who die and kill other humans,' I tried to explain what seemed so obvious to me but, clearly, wasn't apparent to everyone.

'Yes, I guess. I just hadn't thought of it that way before,' admitted the student who was about to become a soldier.

24 The Safest Place in the Army

I felt like I knew that place both extremely well and not at all. I had spent ten years of my childhood right next to it. I watched my friends smoke their first cigarettes near its walls, bunked off lessons in the yard facing it, and every weekday morning, with a mix of curiosity and suspicion, I watched strange creatures in uniform go in and out of the building. The building, its inaccessibility (you could only enter it through a special security gate), its secrecy (it was surrounded by a tall fence; at least it seemed tall to me then), its maleness (almost everyone who went in and out was a man) epitomized, in my impressionable young mind, Sovietness, institutionalism and patriarchy, even if I didn't fully understand these concepts at the time.

The building was the Lviv military commissariat. It was a place where grown-up men in uniform went to work. It was a place where young guys without uniform arrived — often reluctantly — to be dressed in uniform and sent off somewhere where 'they would make men out of them'. And it was a place where mothers came with eyes filled with tears and envelopes filled with banknotes and left without the banknotes but with a feeling of relief that their male offspring would not be 'made into men' somewhere far away from their caring eyes.

I knew that building well, not only because I had a father who had served in the Soviet Army in the 1970s and remained on the reserve list of the new Ukrainian Armed

Forces throughout my childhood, and not only because I had two brothers whom the building had in its sights. I knew it well because my school stood right next to it.

My school was in an excellent location: it was sandwiched between the military commissariat on the one side and a brewery on the other. Both breathed masculinity, and often that breath had the same smell: of cheap alcohol. Both were surrounded by a tall fence and a reception where they checked your ID. And both were merged in my head as places I was not to enter. I wasn't bothered by this restriction on my movement. When you grow up as a girl, you get used to spaces around you being impenetrable simply because of your gender. In any case, I preferred theaters and concert halls, so I was happy to conclude that the boys could have the brewery and the commissariat if they wanted them.

The thing is, however, at least when it came to the military commissariat, the boys didn't really want it. Hence the mothers with their envelopes trying to bribe often impoverished but sometimes just corrupt army officials. Together, they would join in an effort to invent some malady or other reason for a young man to be relieved of his obligatory military conscription.

My mum, like many other good Ukrainian mothers, was ready to do her parental duty and bribe an official to ensure that her firstborn would be spared entering manhood in a uniform that frequently came in a package with bullying, abuse and humiliation. But unlike many of his contemporaries, Volodya really wanted to serve in the army. He really thought that that was the only path to manhood, and so my mother had to accept his wishes and let him be conscripted.

The story, however, took a different turn. Volodya's medical records had an entry that disqualified him from service. An otherwise healthy boy, he had had an episode that made the doctors suspect that he might develop epilepsy. He didn't, but the record stayed. We all forgot about it, but, as is well known, Soviet files do not burn (unless you bribe someone to make sure that they do). The notes resurfaced when Volodya was called up for service. He was told that he wouldn't be able to serve after all.

The distress of a boy eager to become a man is hard to describe. After all the customary fuss of sending a young man off to the army, which involved the entire family and all the family friends being invited to get together as if they were sending him to war in the 1940s, being told that you were not going to serve was more than disappointing. So, now my mum used the envelope she hadn't used to relieve him of his army duty to ensure that his dream of army duty actually came true. To make things even harder for her, Volodya turned out to be an ambitious kid: not only did he want to be conscripted, he wanted to join the Navy. There was no tougher place in the Ukrainian Armed Forces in the 1990s than the Navy. My mum failed. She didn't get him into the Navy. She did, however, manage to secure second-best (or second-worst, depending on your point of view): he was conscripted into the National Guard, which had been created following Ukrainian independence in 1991.

My brother's service coincided with the first 'Crimean crisis': between 1991 and 1994, Ukraine and Russia were dividing the Black Sea fleet between them, and Russia was trying to establish control in the peninsula. It also happened that, during that time, the first Ukrainian-language school was opened in predominantly Russian-speaking Crimea. A group of kids from the Ukrainian-speaking city of Lviv were sent as a delegation to meet the kids in Crimea. I was in that group and got to see the beautiful peninsula for the first time. I remember being driven by a Crimean Tatar, who explained to my mother how hard it was for him and his family to settle there and that he understood Crimean Ukrainians well because they faced a similar type of discrimination. Crimean Tatars had been deported in 1944 by Stalin, having been accused *en masse* of collaboration with the Nazis. It was only in the 1990s that they started to return and reclaim their homes. A kid of nine or so, I didn't fully understand what was going on, but I proudly wore my traditional embroidered shirt and had photos taken of me in it against the exotic sunlit landscapes of beautiful Crimea.

When my brother learned of our little escapade, he was already a soldier in the National Guard. He was furious. I had never heard him speak in such a way to my mother. He phoned her from his unit in Kyiv and told her that our actions were irresponsible, that while we were strolling around in our embroidered shirts, they were ordered to be fully ready for a possible deployment to the sunny peninsula in order to protect Ukrainian territorial integrity. He seemed so concerned for our well-being. Perhaps he was becoming an adult after all. Whether that was because or in spite of the army is another question.

A year and a half later, his service ended, he returned home a sergeant. He had learned the meaning of power and its abuse, of hierarchy and injustice and lots of other things handy when entering adulthood. He also learned that he did not want to become a professional soldier. The army clearly had some work to do in this regard, unless its aim was to permanently discourage the young men it trained from all things connected to the military.

More than two decades after my brother's conscription, he ended up giving his life for Ukraine's territorial integrity. More than two decades after his service as a conscript, the military commissariat from which he had been conscripted was a pitiful sight. Even in my now much more grown-up and less impressionable mind, it still epitomized Sovietness, institutionalism, and patriarchy.

My mum, my partner and I stopped in the reception as we didn't have any IDs that would enable us to enter. I approached the security guard and told him we were there to see Alla Viktorivna. He just waved us through. The place turned out not to be so impenetrable after all.

Walking through the maze of its internal streets, I noticed the paint peeling off the facades of the buildings and the half-torn smiling faces of soldiers and their families on the badly designed recruitment posters. Some bricks in the walls were missing or looked like they were about to go missing. I finally found myself in the inner sanctum I could not enter as a schoolgirl. It resembled the ruins of a temple that had collapsed together with the regime that had erected it.

Alla Viktorivna remembered Volodya well from when he had joined up to serve in the Donbas. She told us how she recalled seeing him sitting in the hall—'There, right there on those chairs'—she pointed to the dilapidated chairs in the corridor outside of her office.

'I said, "Sunshine, you are not registered at this commissariat. You should go to the one where you are registered."'

Sunshine. I don't think any of us ever called him anything remotely resembling 'sunshine,' but this stranger had. 'Sunshine.' I liked hearing her refer to my brother that way.

'But he wouldn't have any of it,' she continued her story. 'He said: "I left to go for my conscription service from here and I'll go to the war from here."'

She gave in. Volodya went to war from their commissariat. Twenty years ago, he convinced one woman—my mother—to do everything in her power to make sure he would go to the army on his terms, and twenty years later he did the same to another.

Alla Viktorivna shouldered the emotional labor of talking and listening to us, bereaved family members, and tried to console us as we walked along the halls of the commissariat to the office of Oleh, the officer who had met us in the airport before the funeral a year earlier. He was wearing the same uniform as all those men who had disappeared behind the tall fence in my childhood. I noticed that it suited him. Once he had greeted us, his rather friendly face — uncommon for a soldier — adopted the austere look that was familiar to me from the day he met us off the plane. He must have been trained to adopt that sort of face, or maybe it comes naturally after meeting a few families like ours to break the news of the loss of their loved one.

He addressed my mother in an official tone that matched his official facial expression:

'I present you with this medal for bravery which was awarded to your son posthumously.'

He passed a little box with a medal inside it to my mum. He also showed us an entry about my brother in a memorial publication. This was already the third volume in this series. It wouldn't be the last. We all fell silent. We were all struggling to hold back our tears.

Where does one keep a medal that is awarded posthumously? It's not the same as your kid's swimming trophy or drawing competition certificate. You don't put it on the mantelpiece or hang it on a wall. Perhaps you just bury it, somewhere in a drawer. Somewhere it can go together with your heartache, with your memories, with your love.

The silence went on for too long, so I decided to say something.

'You know, I wrote a play about Volodya. His death. Well, his life too. Would you be interested in seeing it?'

As I spoke, I realized that Alla Viktorivna and Oleh must be thinking, 'What on earth is she on about? What play?' But they both said: 'Of course!'

'Send it to me via Viber,' Alla Viktorivna added, 'and I'll forward it to Oleh.'

'Why don't you just give me your work email addresses and I'll email the video to you both, and maybe you'll be able to watch it here with other colleagues,' I suggested. I pointed to the computer on an old wooden desk.

'Ah, no, we won't be able to watch it here,' Alla Viktorivna replied, pointing to the same computer. 'I can only read emails at home or on my phone. The military commissariat is not wired to the internet.'

I couldn't believe what I was hearing. In a country where every café has Wi-Fi, often unprotected by a password and faster than the broadband I have at home in London, the military commissariat staff use their private phones to stay in touch with people like us, and read their emails when they get home from work.

'But not having the internet might not be such a bad thing,' Alla Viktorivna added in her usual cheerful manner. 'That means that we are not afraid of a cyber-attack by the enemy.'

We all laughed. Indeed. When it came to cyber-attacks, this must have been the safest place in the army.

I sent Alla Viktorivna the link to the recording of my show about Volodya via Viber. Maybe she watched it at home. Maybe even with her husband, who was a high-ranking professional soldier. Maybe even with her son who had recently returned from the frontline, thankfully, alive.

25 Cozy Grave

'Do you know how you can make these flowers last longer?' a woman asked me as I was fiddling with a pot of flowers I had just bought.

'No, can you tell me? Whatever I bring here always goes dry quickly. It would be great to be able to make them last.'

She proceeded to explain the strategy, but it turned out to be too complicated for my non-gardening brain. Eventually she lost patience and said: 'Look, come with me and I will show you how it's done on another grave.'

We walked from grave to grave discussing plants, pots and methods of keeping them alive. In this place for the dead the conversation about prolonging life, albeit that of flowers, was refreshing.

'So, basically, you cut half of a large plastic bottle off and sit your plant inside it. That way it will have more water and will last longer. The little bowls they give you in shops just don't do the trick on graves. They might work at home on a windowsill but not on a slab of granite.'

The woman showed me exactly how to do it. I said I'd try, although I wasn't sure I would, as I have never been very good at these things.

'You know, I've been in every shop looking to buy something nicer for this purpose, so that it's not a chopped off bottle, but actually something that looks pretty. But they don't have such things! I don't understand why. I am actual-

ly thinking of ordering a special pot for this grave from Po-
land.'

She pointed to the grave next to us. It belonged to a famous soldier who had left a high-profile career as an opera
singer in Western Europe to come and fight the war in
Ukraine.

'Are you related?' I asked carefully, knowing how hard
these questions can be.

'No,' she said and fell silent.

'No' was too short an answer for such a talkative woman, but I felt uncomfortable pursuing the topic, so I told myself that it was none of my business what the relationship
between the woman and the dead soldier was. We continued talking about plants.

'You see these marigolds? They like a lot of water. A lot
of earth. Since I can't plant them here because there is no
earth to plant them in directly on the grave, I made these
special pots for them. See how deep they are?'

I had noticed the manicured pots with marigolds earlier
and often wondered who looked after them, because they
surely must have required a lot of care to remain in such
good condition. Now I knew who it was, and I could no
longer resist asking more about her connection to the grave
with the marigolds.

'I have no connection. No one I know is buried here. No
one I know is fighting in the war. It's just that at one point I
started coming here and looking after this grave. Then I got
to know the relatives of this soldier and others around him.

And now I have met you. We're like a small community here. I don't even know how I used to live not knowing these people.'

I didn't know how to respond to this, so she continued with her monologue.

'You know, it's really terrifying when you read in the news that a grave in such-and-such place was vandalized. You wake up and think: what if *your* grave gets vandalized?' She said this with genuine concern reflected in her face.

'*Your* grave?' I asked cautiously.

'I mean the one I look after,' she clarified. 'I calm myself and say: It won't happen to mine, because there is CCTV here. But then I think: CCTV alone might not be enough! It would be great if they installed a webcam here. That way you could go online any time of day and look at the grave live.'

Again, I didn't respond. I couldn't think of what to say. I kept asking myself why a woman who had no relatives or friends in this cemetery not only came to look after the graves several times a week, but also wanted to be able to check on them online. Didn't she have better things to do? Didn't she have a life to live?

All in black, this woman seemed to have adopted a soldier's grave as if it were that of her partner or a family member. I couldn't get my head around it: I had a genuine reason to be in mourning, and I was putting so much effort into moving on, not getting stuck in grief. But here was a woman who hadn't lost anyone in this war and seemed to embrace a grief that didn't belong to her so willingly that she made it her own.

Sensing my bewilderment, or maybe judgment, my new acquaintance explained herself further: 'This webcam would be good for people like you! You don't live here, do you?' (People in Ukraine can usually spot someone who lives abroad immediately). 'You probably can't come here often. You could just go online and see how the grave is doing.'

How the grave is doing. I knew that, strange as it sounded, deep down I would quite like to go online wherever I was and see how the grave was doing. Since my brother was buried, I've had this overpowering desire to visit his grave. I longed to see it, to spend time there, to light the candles, to bring fresh flowers, to clean the granite, to make it cozy. I knew that 'cozy' was not exactly what a grave should be. Especially not a military grave, with its uniform gravestone, austere gold inscription about military rank, place and manner of death, and the obligatory 'eternal memory to the hero!' line. But I didn't go there to visit a military hero. I went to visit my brother. And I wanted his grave to be cozy.

When I received the drawings of the future gravestone from the architect in charge of the military pantheon, I was horrified by the prospect of my brother being forever militarized: with a photo in a uniform against the dark granite, my brother's multitalented and complex personality would be permanently reduced to that of a soldier. I wasn't sure he would object to it. He had tried on many roles and occupations in his life and seemed very comfortable in his most recent incarnation as a warrior. But I objected to it because I knew that there was so much more to him than this.

After consulting with my family, I decided to demilitarize the grave somewhat by giving it a little civilian makeover. The architect told us that we could engrave something of our choice on the back of the gravestone. I had seen this on other gravestones near my brother's. Some had passages from the Bible on them, the most popular being the line from the Gospel of John: 'There is no greater love than to lay down one's life for one's friends.' Others had an almost life-size picture of the fallen soldier in full military gear. There were some that had a message from the family expressing their sorrow.

I decided to use this bit of stone to remind myself and others that my brother was also an artist. I picked my favorite drawing by him and had it engraved on the back of the gravestone. It depicted a wizard-like man walking in the middle of nowhere, a cat beside him, an eagle in flight above him and a long path behind him. So, now I could look at my brother-the-warrior, the one I didn't know all that well, when I faced the grave, and when I walked behind it, I could see my brother-the-artist, the one I knew as well as one could know such a complicated person. I felt that some balance had been restored.

I understood that, in my wish to civilianize the grave, pretty it up whenever I could and spend so much time there, I was just as peculiar as my new acquaintance with her marigold obsession. The person whose bones were under the granite most probably couldn't care less if the grave was cozy or if the flowers lasted. It was she and I who needed 'our graves' to be cozy.

'You know, they hold a prayer here once a month. And sometimes officials come to lay flowers on the graves and so on,' said the woman.

I nodded. I didn't tell her that I wasn't a big fan of these official rituals. They were certainly more for the benefit of the politicians who held them than the dead who served as a backdrop.

'Well, I get quite upset that the soldiers that stand guard during these events don't get as far as our graves. It is not right that they position themselves only near the center of the pantheon and don't come to these rows. All graves should be honored, don't you think?' she said with some frustration.

I nodded again. Watching news footage of officials' visits to the military pantheon, I had noticed that they didn't quite reach the rows in which my brother's grave was located. Part of me felt frustrated, because that would have given me the chance to see 'how the grave was doing,' but mostly I was pleased that my brother—at least in death—was not being used in someone's PR campaign. I liked it that he was left in peace.

'Are you from Lviv?' she kept our conversation going.

'Yes,' I answered.

'Did your brother live here or abroad?' she persevered.

'Abroad.'

'You see, people just don't understand why anyone would want to leave their comfortable lives abroad and go to the frontline. I tell them: it's because of patriotism! But they don't get it!'

I chose not to tell her that she 'didn't get it' either. That my brother didn't swap a comfortable life for the trenches, that life abroad can also be uncomfortable, that patriotism isn't the only thing that drives people to go to war, and that one can be patriotic without going to the front.

I listened to her talk about self-sacrifice and remembered another acquaintance I had made by my brother's grave a few months earlier on my previous visit. As I was doing my usual thing, wiping the dust off the granite, fussing around the flowers, and replacing old candles with new ones, I felt someone's gaze on me. I turned around and saw a young man on one of the benches not far from the grave. He was drinking beer. It was 4 p.m. on a Tuesday. I decided to approach him.

'Are you here to visit someone you know?' I realized that I had worded the question incorrectly, but it made sense to me, because I visited my brother, not his grave.

'No,' he said. 'But I served in the same battalion as these guys.'

My brother's battalion.

'Did you know my brother? Did you meet him? Were you there at the same time?' I fired question after question in the hope that I had found someone living from the world that to me had become the world of the dead. But he said that he had never met my brother. He was demobilized shortly before my brother joined the battalion. He was lucky. He had survived the war. He could now sit here and drink his beer.

I asked him what he had been doing since he had returned to civilian life.

'Nothing. No one will have me. They think we're not right in the head. They are scared of us. People don't want to hire veterans. They think we can just lose it and kill everyone or something.'

He didn't look like he'd be capable of killing anyone, but of course, he was, or he had been. He had spent a long time on the frontline, and since returning to civilian life he hadn't received any psychological counselling. He showed me a message on his phone inviting him to attend a rally by a politician who was just beginning his electoral campaign.

'They want us to vote for them, but they won't do anything for us. I know it's not up to them to give us jobs or whatever, but I don't like going to these meetings. I prefer coming here.'

He did look peaceful sitting on the bench and drinking his beer. His eyes were so blue, so serene. I could remember them well even several months later. I was wondering what he was doing while I looked into the gray eyes of the marigold woman who was telling me how to prolong the life of flowers. I noticed that her eyes were also peaceful.

I said goodbye to her and went back to the grave to have a few more minutes with my brother. I looked into my make-up mirror and noticed rings of mascara mixed with tears around my brown eyes; I also noticed that they looked a little more peaceful than usual.

On the fifth anniversary of his death, and a month after Russia began its full-scale invasion of Ukraine, I longed to be nowhere other than by my brother's grave. I wanted to make myself busy arranging flowers on the granite and maybe even planting the marigolds the way I was shown a few years earlier. I was hoping to tame my new grief for my country by focusing on the grief for my brother. But I had no means of travelling to my home town, which now found itself in a warzone, and to the grave, which truly felt as if it now belonged to another, inaccessible world.

Crying in my London flat, unable to rein in my emotions, I saw a picture message appear on my phone. It showed my brother's grave. A bunch of willow stems with furry buds, a sign of spring, lay on the granite. Next to the bouquet was a note: 'From Olesya. 24.03.2022' A message from a friend who had left London for Ukraine a few weeks before the full-scale invasion followed the photo: 'I didn't ask if you liked willow or if Volodya did. But I figured that it was the sort of bouquet that was both austere and spring-like.' She continued: 'It's calm here.' My home town was still relatively safe, but it was being targeted by Russian missiles at the time, as was the whole of the country. Nowhere in Ukraine was totally calm. But maybe the cemetery was. 'The grave is cozy,' she said at the end of her message.

26 Spring

I have looked at the videos of the snow-covered trench, the lake beside it and the frozen drops of rain so many times that I feel that I have visited that ill-fated place myself. I even started to share the fondness for it my brother projected so palpably in the videos I found in his phone. The beauty and serenity of the place seemed so unsuited as the setting for a warzone. But peace and war, serenity and violence can exist side by side whether among humans or in the natural world.

When the snow starts to fall everything falls silent. The crumbled diamonds drop from the sky and settle into a soft quilt, bonding with the layer beneath and waiting for others like them to form a layer above. Coat after coat of utter stillness. Of sparkling whiteness. Of soundless peace. From above, the winter landscape of the eastern Ukrainian steppe looks like one expansive duvet whose promise of warmth lures you into the inward cold. You dive into it and fall asleep forever.

It's only from above that the sheet of whiteness looks completely serene and lifeless. Inside, it is full of suspended animation, somewhere between life and death. The mice stay pretty active: they build whole galleries in the snow. They are joined by voles who make dens in the depths of white. There, they pass the winter months hidden from predators. Or so it would seem. A weasel, hungry for food in the middle of winter, is capable of crawling through the tunnels they have constructed. A place built for safety turns into a labyrinth of deadly pursuit.

A vixen, dressed for the weather, is able to hunt unhindered by the cold. She ventures out at night, picking the smaller and larger rodents right out of their nests and making them her dinner. She has an excellent sense of smell. All she has to do is scent the fear of the little beasts beneath her, bury her face into the snow and, in a flash, the prey is in her teeth.

Some creatures refuse to give in to predators, regardless of how much smaller or weaker they might be. A late-nesting bird will protect its precious eggs by all means available to it: even if all it is able to do in the face of danger is sing as loudly as it can.

A hedgehog, on the other hand, tries to hibernate to avoid witnessing all these horrors. A hare, not the bravest of animals, keeps a low profile during the day to avoid trouble and comes out only at night to find food and get a bit of exercise. But this cautious behavior does not necessarily protect these creatures from danger. A few hours after sunset, the eagle-owl comes out to hunt. Its orange eyes are sharp, its long claws ready to inflict fatal damage. It watches its victim from a branch and then plunges down, grabs the doomed animal with its talons and crushes it to death. The only consolation for the prey is that death is usually quick. Once the victim is killed, it is swallowed whole or torn to pieces and consumed bit by bit. And all that remains are the drops of red on the otherwise perfect white.

Different hunters adopt different techniques to make their living. Rather than rummaging in the snow or patiently waiting for a good moment to attack from the sky, the wolves unite their forces, and, in packs, wander into villages to attack vulnerable domestic cattle. Where there is unity there is strength. And if you don't have much between the ears and don't take any precautions to stay safe, whose fault is it that you fall prey to a hungry pack of wolves?

But let's come back to the duvet of cold. To peace and quiet. To winter. The best thing about it is that sooner or later it ends. The ice melts in the sun, revealing the life beneath it. And as the white, here and there stained with red, vanishes, the black below emerges. But it doesn't stay black for long. The dormant green shoots awaken, sensing the change in the air, they sprout through the earth and out into the world, eager to see the rays of the sun for themselves. When the heavy clouds return, admitting that their days are numbered, and pour their grief out onto the earth, what falls is no longer sharp and icy. It is nourishing. The raindrops land on the thirsty soil, they make puddles for the birds to bathe in.

On its way out, winter breathes a bit of frost over its shoulder, not to frighten anyone, but to leave a little parting gift behind. The drops of rain suspended in mid-descent, turn into shiny diamonds that adorn the branches of the trees, still black, but only until the green buds appear on them and the new life begins. Until spring. Not long now.

27 The Flat. Your Flat

It's really handy that our flat in Lviv is not very far from the cemetery. I can walk there in twenty minutes or even less. And it's mostly a pleasant walk. There is one junction where the cars don't bother stopping even though there is a crossing there, but otherwise, once you leave the cemetery, you walk through some quiet, leafy residential streets, up a hill, and then you are home.

Home. How strange it is for me to think of having a home in this city again. For nearly twenty years, we had no home here. We sold our flat before we emigrated. We never thought we'd be able to buy something here again. And, to be honest, we never really saw the point. Whenever I returned to my home town, I mostly came on business and either stayed in hotels paid for by conference organizers or, if I came on a research trip, I rented a little apartment somewhere far from the flat in which I grew up. I didn't even like passing my old flat. I didn't want to see the familiar sights, smell the familiar smells, and have memories flood back in. I was happy being a tourist, a visitor. Or so I told myself.

When my brother died, my mother was contacted by the municipal authorities and told that she was entitled to some sort of compensation. They didn't call it that. As with most war-related terms, there is a euphemism for it: 'a one-off payment,' or something like that. It was a sizable sum, around £10,000. When we heard this, my mother and I agreed that we didn't want it. It wasn't that we were so wealthy that £10,000 meant nothing to us. Not at all. It's more that any sum of money offered as 'compensation' for your loved one's life just seemed wrong. Of course, the logic behind this 'one-time payment' is to help the family get back on its feet when the main breadwinner – and that is who servicemen and women usually are – is no longer able to provide for them.

They told my mother that, whether she wanted it or not, they would issue the money to her, and she could then do as she pleased with it. My mother thought about it and agreed to accept it, provided Liuba, the woman who'd been our guardian angel during the funeral, would help us find a trustworthy charity the sum could be donated to. And that is what happened. The £10,000 arrived in my mother's account and was transferred immediately to a charity that supported sick children. Each month my mother would get a little report with photos of smiling children who were doing better and better, successfully battling cancer or some other serious and expensive illnesses. The money she donated meant that they could get the medication they had not been able to afford but badly needed. The joy on my mother's face when she looked at those photos is hard to convey. I guess it was a compensation of sorts for my brother's loss after all.

But then another phone call came. This time the officials were telling my mother that, as she didn't own any property, she was entitled to a one-bedroom flat as a parent of a fallen soldier. Now, that was even more of a shock. Who would have thought that such things were possible in a poor country like Ukraine? This time we didn't think of rejecting the offer. We accepted it and ended up with a small flat, located in a converted 1950s Soviet building. Apparently, in the period that the building served as housing for workers, the flat had been used as the 'Red Corner': the mandatory room, found in all institutions, filled with propaganda material, pictures of General Secretaries and other Soviet paraphernalia. When I went inside for the first time, I tried to imagine where the bust of Lenin might have sat, where the obligatory red banner would have been hung, and where the dreary socialist realist books might have been stored to be distributed to the workers to convert them into real communists.

This was quite a change from the flat in which my brothers and I grew up. Located in an old Austro-Hungarian tenement building in the city center, it had high ceilings and thick walls, and you could never imagine a bust of Lenin or a red banner as part of its interior. But I didn't care that this new flat of ours was an old Soviet hostel. The most important thing about it was that it was so near the cemetery that I could go and visit the grave early in the morning as I left the flat to go on business, or in the evening as I made my way home.

Home. I had a home in my city once more. I had it because my brother didn't need one anymore.

As none of us live in Lviv permanently, the flat would stay empty between our fleeting visits. This made me quite sad. I didn't want our home to be empty. But then, one day, a childhood friend of my brother's said that his son was moving to Lviv to study at the university. He had been given a place in the halls of residence in a room with ten other boys on a floor with one shower. My mother immediately invited the young man to stay in the flat instead. This, too, felt like a certain kind of compensation. In the period when my brother had been sleeping rough, it was this friend of his—the father of the student—who had looked after him, brought him food and patiently put up with his demons. He had stayed a good friend right until the end. It only made sense for his son now to benefit from the kindness he had shown to my brother all those years back.

During one visit, I found myself in the flat on my own for the first time. My father had made it quite comfortable, having painted the walls and bought the necessary furniture. But each time I had stayed there before I felt a sense of unease. I had felt like I had been staying at my brother's while he was away. Now that I was there by myself, I could finally face up to my emotions. I made myself a cup of tea, sat down on the sofa, and started speaking to my brother as if he were there, having a cup of tea with me. I told him that all this was so messed up and that I really couldn't get my head around it, but that I was grateful to him for gifting this home to us. I described what the flat was like, that it used to serve as a 'Red Corner' in the olden days, how I liked it that it was so close to him, to his grave, and that it was within walking distance of the city center, which he loved so much.

I finished my tea, dried my face down which the tears had poured and poured as I held this imaginary conversation with my brother, and went to bed. That was the first time I slept right through the night in that flat. When I got up in the morning, I felt a sense of relief. I had a quick coffee and briskly walked to the cemetery through the quiet residential streets. It didn't even take me twenty minutes.

When, in 2022, the attack by Russia pushed Ukrainians from east and south to the western regions of the country, we offered our flat to internally displaced people. At one point, it housed seven people, a dog and a cat. Those escaping death and destruction found shelter in a flat that had been given to the family of a fallen soldier. Amidst the horror of an all-out war, it warmed my heart to know that a free man, now dead, was hosting free people from different parts of his free country.

28 What Remains

I can't visit my brother's grave often. I only go to my home town a couple of times a year. I don't like making shrines in my flat with photos of relatives displayed for all to see. But I do feel the need to honor my brother's memory in some way in the privacy of my home now and again. I have this folder where my brother kept his papers, and where I now keep all the paperwork related to his time in the war. I sometimes take the folder out of the bookcase, place it in front of me, and go through the documents one by one.

As soon as I open it, a distinct smell emerges out of it and envelops me until I get used to it and stop noticing it. It is hard to describe it as anything other than the smell of a life that once was. It's a blend of aging papers, the earth, old plastic, and memories.

To all the documents my brother had collected, I added his death certificate. So, now it is next to his birth certificate. These two pieces of paper bracket his entire life, but actually say little about it. There are also paintings and drawings that he made. One of them depicts a couple facing a strange spirit all in white with only a red tongue sticking out of its fanged mouth. It is holding a scythe. The couple stand calmly in front of the creature: the man is dressed in a suit, his brown hair down to his shoulders and the woman is wearing a long red coat, her hair, which reaches down to her waist, is an even brighter red than her coat. Above that scene, there is another. This time the same couple is framed by an explosion of colors that lie in front of them. They are about to step into what looks like the starlit sky. I like to open the folder and look at his drawings. But they also awaken a sense of frustration: why didn't he just keep painting? Why did he have to go to the frontline?

The folder also contains the business cards that were given to me by local politicians outside the morgue and even by the graveside on the day of the funeral. I keep them as reminders that wars and funerals are part of someone's business.

Apart from the papers, the most important thing I have is my brother's phone. I also keep it in the folder now. When I decided to look at its contents for the first time, I found text messages which were addressed to me, but which never reached me. It turned out that he had tried to get in touch more often than I had imagined. It's just that the messages weren't always able to travel out of the warzone. I sometimes feel like replying to them, hoping that this would complete our many incomplete conversations.

In his phone, I also found photos he took in the warzone of dugouts, weapons, ruined buildings, men and women I didn't know, and even a kitten. There were also photos of a dead body, a skeleton in a uniform that had clearly been found in the tall grass by some soldiers, who also appeared in the photos. A kitten sitting on a rifle, a skeleton in the tall grass, a beautiful lake that could well have been surrounded by a minefield: that's the sort of photo gallery you can find on a soldier's phone. These photos always raised more questions than they answered. What did all this mean to my brother? Was the world of the war really his world? Were the people in the photos able to become his new family? How did a man who had always had long hair feel having a shaved head? How did he feel wearing khaki? Was he scared of getting killed? Was he afraid of being a part of the killing machine?

When I sit down with the folder in front of me and look through the documents, letters, videos, pictures and texts I realize that they don't help me remember my brother's life. Because what remains is mostly gaps, and I have to fill them with my own words. I sit and think about what really remains now that he's gone: Is it the hatred I feel towards those who profit where lives are lost? Is it the kindness that people express when they hear my brother's story? Or is it just a huge gap that could only ever be filled by my strange, talented and absolutely infuriating brother?

29 The Enemy

> 'To suffer in chains is a great humiliation, but to forget those chains
> without having broken them is the worst kind of shame.'
> Lesia Ukrainka

I don't hate them. I don't hate the Russians as a nation. I wish I could because it would provide an outlet for my pain, grief and rage. I sometimes envy my friends who can spit out abuse towards the enemy like you'd spit out rotten fruit. This hate-filled rejection of an entire people seems to liberate them. But I can't do it.

When the Russians started the full-scale invasion, it was 3am in London. I was awake finishing an article I had promised to send to a newspaper by the morning. I decided to check Twitter one more time before going to bed. Lightning symbols at the start of tweets did not just signal breaking news, they signalled explosions. Scrolling through my feed, I came across a video in which a CNN correspondent standing in front of Kyiv's majestic St Sophia bell tower was reporting live that he had just heard 'a big bang right here behind me'. Another journalist, a former US Army veteran who had been reporting on the war in Ukraine since 2014 and kept warning about the escalation, tweeted: 'Good God it's actually happening'.

Just as on the day when I learned that my brother had been killed, I had a clear mind and acted methodically. I picked up the phone and called my closest friend, who had just gone back to Ukraine a couple of weeks earlier. She

hadn't felt like doomscrolling on her London sofa and preferred to make herself useful in Ukraine in case it 'actually
happened'. Realizing that at 5am Kyiv time she'd probably
still be asleep, I rang until she picked up. How do you wake
someone up to tell them that their country's under attack? I
tried to put on my gentlest voice, like the one my mother
would use when she woke me up on a dark winter morning
to get me ready for school.

'Wake up, my dear, it's started,' I said.

'So, it's actually happening then?' She replied half asking for clarification, half confirming to herself that she had
made the right choice and wouldn't be doomscrolling from
London like I was.

I then called my London friends whose families I knew
to be in Kyiv, to let them know that 'it was happening'.
Having done my duty as a messenger of bad news, I descended onto the floor in the middle of the living room, still
holding on to my phone, and started to howl like I had done
when the news of my brother's death hit me properly for
the first time.

'Damn you! All of you,' I heard myself say out loud. I
have never cursed anyone in my life until then. The words
were made of such profound darkness that I didn't even
know I could carry something like that inside me. They
were directed at the Russians. Not only Putin. Not simply
the ones who were launching the rockets. The entire nation.
The power of the words uttered into an empty living room
was so strong that I could feel the vibrations of my own

voice against my skin. The darkness was so heavy that it enveloped me entirely and began to suffocate me.

I was terrified of the might of my curse. At that moment, I was certain that my wish for them all to be damned was just and would therefore come true. The bright book-filled living room started to go dark as if someone had dimmed the lights, and kneeling in the middle of it on the floor with my phone in my hands, I felt as if I was falling into the abyss. I was being crushed under the weight of my curse.

In my mind, I recited the names of those whom I could ring and ask for support as one recites a prayer memorized in early childhood. I stopped at Masha. Of course. Who else? We had just spoken an hour or so ago, having not been in touch for several months because of our busy lives. Then—which now felt like a lifetime ago—she had asked me what the mood was like in the UK. I said that everyone was pretty sure the full-on war was imminent. I asked her what she thought. She too agreed that it was imminent. 'It might not happen tonight, but it will happen soon', she said. It did happen that night. I phoned her back and like a child said: 'Masha, what do I do now? What is the most efficient thing to do?' She told me to get in touch with journalists and raise the alarm.

The next few weeks became a haze of giving interviews, talks, comments by day and checking the news and breaking into fits of crying by night. Until my tears dried up and the only thing that remained was a desperate need to be efficient. Unlike my friends and relatives in Ukraine, I didn't have to work from a bomb shelter. I could sleep in my own bed. I was not in danger of being raped by the invading troops. My parents were not at risk of being taken out of their homes and shot in the back of their heads. My partner or my brother hadn't been called up. My eldest brother had been killed in this war, but he had been buried in a beautiful cemetery, not in a mass grave. I counted my blessings one after another to keep myself going and stay efficient. Curses were not efficient, so they were left behind in the darkness of my living room, in the middle of the floor.

Do I still want them all to be damned? I don't dare answer that question. I just know I am not able to hate them all.

I despise the ones who endorsed their criminal regime through silence. I loathe those who remained 'apolitical', letting blood pour through their fingers but saying 'we didn't cause the bleeding, so it's not our fault'. I can't tolerate the ones who do not feel complicit in the war because they are against-Putin-and-want-peace. Paying taxes that fund the army won't bring about peace, so those who choose to continue their lives in Russia as normal must at least be aware of their complicity. I pity the rest who have grown accustomed to living in humiliation, contempt, injustice administered by their own government. I have no respect for those for whom dignity is as alien as freedom.

Do I hate the Russian army? Can a group of looting, raping thugs be called an army? I feel repulsion when I think of criminals whose 'army duty' consisted of shooting civilians, torturing children and sharing their 'conquests' with supportive relatives back in their police state. Those who joined up having been persuaded that they were going to 'de-Nazify' Ukraine were just as criminal as their looting comrades. Some of them realized they had been wrong when they got to Ukraine and saw no Nazis, only the hatred in the eyes of Russophone Ukrainians for their murdering 'liberators'. Ignorance is a choice. The choice they made when, for years, they lapped up propaganda and again when they set off to 'bring peace' by shelling hospitals and kindergartens.

There's also another type: the ones stricken by poverty. When, following the collapse of the USSR, Ukrainians kept on fighting the corrupt legacy of the old Communist empire and tried their best to grow into democracy, Putin's Russia perfected repression and poverty, developing a nation so docile it was frightened to imagine a life without its abusive leader. Those soldiers who signed their contracts to kill Ukrainians in order to make a bit of money for their families in the most deprived regions of Russia—the regions that often happen to be populated by national minorities—film their excitement at the sight of a Nutella jar in one of the Ukrainian flats they plundered. Not to mention the stolen washing machines that have now become an emblem of Russian 'conquests'. This pathetic scene fails to spur hatred in me. I simply want them gone from my country, all of them, the poor, the ideological, the cynical.

The Russians do not take to the streets to protest the war because the media is censored in Russia, say some. It's because people are afraid to make their voices heard, explain others. Putin is to blame. Not the Russians. But it's the Russians who shaped Putin as much as he shaped Russia. He put the chains on them, and they wore them obediently.

But what about the ones who opposed? The ones who left Russia because they did not agree with the regime? Some declare their disgust with the war and say that it is not conducted in their name, but still choose to post on their social media platforms a picture of their granddad with the ribbon of St George—the current symbol of violence against Ukrainians—on 9th May. Others, in London, Berlin or Vienna, publicly join 'Victory Day' parades that have long stopped serving the function of commemorating the war dead and have instead been turned into the frenzy of the Russian cult of violence.

There are those who openly speak of their complicity through sheer association with the aggressor and do what they can to help stop the war. But they are so few and far between in a nation of 140 million that they serve as exceptions that prove the rule. Before the full-scale invasion, their presence used to reassure me that not all is lost in Russia. Now, their miniscule numbers simply make me feel sorry for them. Being Russian and fully realizing what pain that nationality has come to symbolise to so many can't be easy.

And Putin? The only image my mind conjures up when I hear that name is, no, not of his grave, but of familiar pho-

tos from the Nuremberg trials but with him and his entou-
rage in the dock in place of the Nazis. My mind photoshops
their faces into the historic photos to remind me that justice
prevails. Yes, it is partial, delayed, incommensurate with the
suffering caused by the perpetrators, but I want to believe
that it will be administered, and that we will see that image
everywhere as we have been seeing the images of the mass
graves from Irpin, Bucha, Mariupol.

If I could hate the entire nation that has chosen to become my enemy, my new grief, now not just for my brother,
but for my whole people, might pour out, and I might be
able to live without the need to carry its weight wherever I
go.

But I don't. I don't hate all Russians, but nor do I feel
sympathy or forgiveness. While my feelings evolve, the one
thing that will not change is the desire for justice. And I
know it will come.

30 An Opportune Moment

Things have changed since the full-scale invasion of Ukraine. On 24 February 2022, the contours of the map of Ukraine lit up on TV screens all over the world. The country was being placed on the mental map of viewers who were watching Ukrainian cities and towns being bombed more or less live. The journalists who had been sent to Ukraine a few months prior, as the Russian troops had been swarming around the country's borders, finally had the picture they came for: explosions on the horizon of the ancient city of Kyiv, a capital city so similar to the ones from which their viewers were watching these war reports.

When I first arrived in the UK, most locals didn't have a clue where Ukraine was and the knowledge of those who did was limited to Chornobyl and Shevchenko. Not the 19th-century Romantic poet, the founder of the nation, Taras Shevchenko, but Andrii Shevchenko, a footballer who was popular at the time. When the Orange Revolution happened in 2004, the map of Ukraine briefly appeared on TV screens of westerners. Reporters who were frequently based in Moscow and had little knowledge of the country they were actually reporting on painted Ukraine as split between pro-Europeans and pro-Russians. In 2014, Ukraine's life on the western screens was more prolonged than ten years earlier, but the narratives were still oversimplified and heavily influenced by Russian propaganda attempts to discredit Ukrainians' fight against authoritarianism.

Ukraine continued to be misunderstood. It was just too complex to get one's head around, and, at the same time, there was no pressing need to get one's head around it. The occupation of Crimea and Russian aggression in the Donbas brought Ukraine back into newsrooms. As Ukrainians kept losing lives in the fight for their territorial integrity, they were gaining clarity of vision about the country they were building with blood, sweat and tears. But, having expressed its deep concern, the world moved on. Ukraine fatigue descended. Until the full-scale invasion of February 2022 when things began to change, and the world decided it was time to discover this terra incognita.

'You've been in touch with us before with some ideas for collaboration on a project on Ukraine, haven't you?' I heard this question from the program manager of yet another important western cultural institution that had decided to do an event on Ukraine but had quickly figured out that it didn't have in-house expertise to make sure that they got it right at such a sensitive time.

'That was me, yes', I responded. 'But it didn't seem to have worked out for you then,' I added cautiously, trying to make a point but not wishing to offend.

'It didn't. Well, that's because...' My interlocutor looked for the words to explain why a project on Ukraine had not seemed timely for their organisation a year or so ago, the last time we spoke. Ukraine was not trending then. There was no war on, right?

Except there *was* a war on. But we, in Western Europe, could afford to ignore it to the point that we seemed to have persuaded ourselves that Russia's war in Ukraine began on 24 February 2022.

The cultural institution I was talking to could no longer afford to ignore the war, if not because it was claiming so many more lives and threatening security in Europe as a whole, then because it would look bad when other similar institutions had done an event on Ukraine but theirs hadn't.

'It didn't work out last time, that's true. But now is an opportune moment', said my interlocutor.

An opportune moment. So that is what the war was for them. In many ways it was true. Wars can present opportunities for change that seem impossible in peacetime: from granting rights to women (at least some rights to some women), to changing migration policies to accommodate war refugees (at least some refugees), to introducing sanctions against an aggressor (at least some sanctions). Those opportunities tend to come at a very high cost though. The cost is measured in people's lives.

Before 24 February 2022, Russia's aggression had already caused much destruction, pain and grief: nearly two million Ukrainians had been displaced, mostly internally, so the EU didn't need to worry about accommodating them. Seven per cent of the territory of Ukraine had been occupied by Russia, which meant that people in Crimea and the Donbas were living in constant threat of being kidnapped, tortured or murdered if they opposed the regime or if the thugs in charge of their cities decided that they wished to appropriate their flats, cars or businesses. Thousands had been killed. None of that was enough to bring about change.

Towns and cities razed to the ground, thousands of civilians killed by shelling or shot in the head at close range, thousands more tortured, injured, made homeless. Millions displaced within Ukraine and in the EU. That seemed to be sufficient to bring the world's attention to Ukraine. The size of the loss, it turns out, matters when it comes to opportune moments.

I had the urge to say all of this when speaking to the cultural institution's program manager. When I was asked to explain the country that no longer fit into the image of a god-forsaken, corrupt 'post-Soviet space', with its people who displayed defiance when they were expected to display victimhood, I wanted to ask why Ukraine had been of no interest to them for the last eight years (or the last thirty years). But I didn't. Instead, I asked how I could be of help. I had to recognize that, for Ukraine too, this was an opportune moment.

This was the moment when the situational interest in Ukraine that emerged as a result of Russia's full-scale invasion had to be turned into structural changes. These changes were needed not only to finally get to know Ukraine as it really was and not as Russia presented it, but also to understand the challenges that Russia's aggression presented to the wider world. It was an opportunity for the rest of the democratic world to ask the question that was being an-swered in Ukraine: what is the cost of freedom? This was the moment when having shown the world its resilience, self-reliance and collective strength, Ukraine had to stop being the object of patronizing lecturing and become a sub-ject with experience that was of existential value across the world.

I am not a fan of comparing affairs of states or nations to those between people—for instance, explaining the rela-tionship between Russia and Ukraine through the metaphor of a divorce that's gone badly. But there is something in the way Ukraine has been perceived in the West that I recognize in my personal experience. Being an immigrant and a wom-an, it has always been a struggle to have my voice heard. Sometimes quite literally: to have the courage to raise my hand and ask a question in a Q&A session when all other raised hands were those of older men; to speak with enough confidence so that people listened not to my accent, trying and failing to place it on their mental maps, but to the mean-ing behind my words; to break through a wall of ignorance veiled as superior knowledge. For a long time, I experienced what one of my academic friends described as epistemic mistrust. Referring to the same experience, another friend referred to those of us who had raised the alarm about this war but had not been heard as 'modern-day Cassandras'. That is, we found ourselves in possession of the sort of knowledge that was vital but not desired.

As the doors that had previously been shut began to open, and people who would not have given a second thought to Ukraine began to arrange talk shows, write op-eds and curate exhibitions on the country, they started to look for a 'Ukrainian voice' that could explain to them everything from Volodymyr the Great to Volodymyr Zelensky, preferably in the 5 minutes they had allocated for this and in a form that was accessible. However, while being given the voice, I still felt like someone who was expected to contribute her 'local' knowledge, for instance, to explain how to pronounce an unreasonable combination of consonants in the name of a city such as Zaporizhzhia, or as someone who could talk 'emotionally' and 'passionately' just before the 'real' commentators were brought on to discuss the same issues 'objectively'. While I was being invited to participate in a conversation, I was not being invited to steer it. The familiar epistemic mistrust was turning into epistemic exploitation.

It took a while for me to decide that this was the opportune moment not only to fill the huge gap in the knowledge on Ukraine, but also to shape the questions that I was being asked. To retain attention on Ukraine when the discussion turned to Russia. To promote Ukrainian anti-imperial literature to those who bemoaned the decolonization of Pushkin, Tolstoy, Dostoevsky. To not only encourage the epistemic trust of Ukraine but also reveal the epistemic value of the experience possessed by the country and its people: the country that surprised the world. The international community gave it three days before it would fall to Russian aggression. Instead, we witnessed the unprecedented resilience of the state and astounding defiance of its people.

For those people, the lines from Shevchenko—the poet, not the footballer—were not some dusty words pulled out of a drawer once a year to be recited with pathos beside his monument. Since the 19th century, when they were written, they have served as a call to action. In 2014, when Shevchenko's portrait, creatively dressed as one of the protesters, peeked through barricades on the Maidan, they were reminders that the fight was just. Since February 2022, they are a statement of fact:

> Keep fighting—and you will prevail,
> God himself will aid you!
> Truth and glory stand beside you
> And the holy freedom.

The Ukrainian people have no tradition of venerating their political leaders. Unlike in Russia, politicians lose the support of their disillusioned electorate as soon as they betray their promises. What Ukrainians do revere is freedom. This value of freedom was shaped by the lived experience of generations who were forbidden from speaking their language, or even perceiving it as a language, denied statehood and thus political representation, whose culture was belittled and misunderstood. The culture that expressed the urgency of freedom from external colonizers and internal oppression for the nation's survival. But if it is spoken or recorded in a language that isn't really a language, why bother exploring it? Epistemic mistrust of the entire nation, its people and culture created a gap the size of 230 square miles. About 2.5 times bigger than the UK.

If this gap is filled with everything from Pushkin to Putin, how will the epistemic mistrust be overcome? How will it be understood that for Ukrainians freedom is not something to be taken for granted, like it is for some peoples west of them, or something to be feared, like in the country to the east. It is something to be experienced. As Ukrainians were fighting for their freedom with everything they had, from weapons to words, an opportune moment presented itself for the world to discover what inspired this fight.

31 I Can't Believe You're Dead: A Letter.

[no address]
[no date]

Dear Volodya,
Since I can't believe that you're dead, I decided to write to you directly.

Each time I remember that you are gone, I can't quite believe it. I think: 'That can't be true. He's just gone away again. He's somewhere with poor phone reception. Busy. He can't be bothered to get in touch.' Let's face it, you weren't exactly good at getting in touch when you were alive, so, all this makes sense in my head much more than thinking that you are dead.

I never replied to that letter you sent me years ago. I cherish it dearly and re-read it regularly, but I didn't respond to it partly because I didn't know what to say (a poor excuse, I know) and partly because I didn't know where I should send my reply. You never had a permanent address, if you had one at all. Let this be my belated response. Better late than never, right?

I don't know if you remember what you wrote in your letter, so I will cite it here in full (it's short):

[no address]
[no date]

[no greeting]

I write to you [plural, presumably meaning the entire family, not just me] via email or send you text messages only when I feel really bad, when I am drunk, not myself. That is why you have a (slightly) skewed impression of me.

In general, judging people at a distance can be very dangerous. And unobjective. I know this from personal experience. People who are around me, who see me every day at work and at home, think that I am perfectly normal. Sometimes even more normal than those people who are officially deemed normal.

The point I'm making is that it's not all so bad. Things could be much worse with one's mind and with one's soul. I've seen it. I know.

[A few lines left intentionally blank, for dramatic effect, I assume.]

If we believe in the existence of extreme evil, and I assume that we do believe in it, then we should recognize the existence of the opposite extreme.

Dr House

With your letter, you enclosed one hryvnia, a silly newspaper article about a sex scandal in a nightclub in the Ukrainian town of Kolomyia, and a copy of two of your drawings.

Your drawings make me think of William Blake. They seem to display that same agony of trying to figure out the world around you, and, failing that, striving to invent your own mythology, a different world, one that makes sense in your head. I wonder if you like Blake's work. You probably don't. Or, if you do, you'd say that you don't, just to annoy me.

I keep the letter in its original golden envelope, like one of the little treasures I kept as a kid in a special box. Sometimes I open it to re-read its contents, sometimes just to look at your handwriting — unlike me, you always had such elegant handwriting — and sometimes to remind myself just how 'perfectly normal' you were.

What I never told you, though I suspect you already know, is that I have also sent you texts and emails when I felt particularly bad. I didn't mean so much of what I said. I didn't say so much of what I meant to say.

For the first six months after your funeral, I kept dreaming of you. Those dreams were soothing, comforting and very vivid. The most memorable was this: we were on a bus together. You sat in front of me, wearing your uniform. I reached out to hug you and could almost feel your jacket under my arms. We then heard a group of young men in the seats nearby, also in uniform, talk about something. I asked you if you knew them. You said:

'Oh, those little posh shits! Yeah, they keep messaging me.'

I was aware that none of you were alive and was surprised to hear that you had some means of communication with each other. I just opened my mouth to ask if I could message you too, but you interrupted me saying:

'Don't even think about it!'

And then I woke up.

Mum had a funny dream about you: you were peeling potatoes and she was telling you off for something or other. Suddenly, you turned around and started to recite Lermontov at her! I couldn't stop laughing when she told me her dream. I wonder what poem you recited to her. Did Lermontov write anything about potatoes?

The last time I saw you in a dream you were not wearing your uniform. Mum, dad, Yura and I went to visit your grave. They all popped into the shop to get candles and flowers. But I noticed that you had been waiting for us by the train station and stopped to talk to you. I barely recognized you in your crisp ironed shirt and formal trousers. I don't remember if you ever owned such formal clothes. You seemed impatient. You said:

'I've been waiting here for you all to say goodbye. Tell them to hurry up with their candles and flowers. I don't have long. We are being moved.'

I didn't ask where you were being moved to or by whom. I sort of knew what you meant in the dream and didn't need to clarify it.

It seems that you really did move somewhere, because I haven't dreamt of you since.

You know what I find hardest? Not letting my grief fuel the growth of hatred in me. From the day they told us you were dead, I felt it grow somewhere inside my chest, each day getting a bit bigger, each day eating up something else—love, reason, compassion—to make more space for itself. I felt so powerless against it that I decided to go to confession. Not something I'd normally do, as you know. You're probably laughing reading this. You've never been a big fan of organized religion. But I thought that if 'thou shalt love thy neighbor' is the second greatest commandment then hating your neighbor must be at least among the top ten sins, and priests should know a thing or two about how to resist it.

I never think of the person who pulled the trigger and caused your death. I don't hate him or her. As I hope that some grieving relatives don't hate you for pulling the trigger and maybe causing the deaths of their loved ones.

I do hate the politicians who are quick to return to 'business as usual' at the expense of people's lives. I hate businessmen who make money trading with war criminals. I hate the international community, which I am a part of, that expresses its deep concern so as to cover up its self-interest and inaction.

So, I knelt down, said that it's been years and years since my last confession, and started to go through the inventory of all the people I hated. The priest eventually interrupted my monologue and said:

'It sounds like you really loved your brother.'

I thought it was a strange thing to say to someone who's just been talking about hatred. I said:

'Yes, I really loved him.'

He then said:

'His death need not stop you from loving him. If you focus on love, let it grow in your heart, it won't leave much space for hatred.'

I've tried to do that ever since. It mostly works.

Anyway, I should stop disturbing you. You did tell me in the dream to not even think about getting in touch. I hope you forgive me just this once. I really wanted to tell you that I don't believe that you are dead and that I think it's okay, because you are alive. In my heart, in my thoughts, in my memories.

I don't have a witty quote to end on. So, I'll just say: look after yourself, wherever you are.

Much love.

Yours always,
Olesya

Author's Acknowledgments

I would have preferred not to have had to write this book, to have had no subject matter to write about, to have had my brother alive rather than my book published. But since the subject matter materialized, I am lucky to have been able to commit my reflections to paper, not to submerge them in the depths of my sorrow but to lift my grief line by line, and, by doing so, make my heavy heart a little lighter. I could never have done it alone.

I cannot be grateful enough to my family—my mother Olha, father Yuriy and brother Yura—not only for letting me share these stories, but for actively encouraging me to write them down. After all, these stories do not belong to me alone; each of us might tell them differently, but they are a shared family possession. I thank my partner, Uilleam Blacker, for being there for me in the darkest moments of my grief, for listening to every first draft and reading subsequent drafts of this text attentively and sensitively.

The actors of Molodyi Teatr London, my theater company—Lesya Liskevych, Liliya Romanyshyn, Iryna Sandalovych, Uilleam Blacker, Olga Malchevska, Volodymyr Glushak, Slavko Tsyhan and Fin Ross Russell—allowed me to think through my trauma out loud and created a space in which I could step outside of my own story in order to regard it at some distance, for which I am very thankful. They also offered their trusted friendship and unrelenting sense of humor even at moments when laughter seemed impossible.

I'm blessed with dear friends who are also fellow academics and who were willing to combine their compassion and professional judgment while reading this volume: Julie Fedor and Molly Flynn—thank you! I am immeasurably grateful to Sasha Dovzhyk for lending a sharp eye for detail and a heart full of warmth. A friend who got to know this war first-hand—Maria Berlinska—gave me the confidence to speak of it, even though I was fortunate not to have experienced it myself. To the many other friends and colleagues who patiently listened to me speak about the war in general and my own loss in particular, I will forever be grateful to you for offering your time, support and ideas.

I am touched by the endorsements and support I received for this book. Cynthia Enloe is my heroine when it comes to finding a sensitive approach to individuals' experiences of political violence. I am moved by how sincerely Anna Reid cares for the welfare of Ukraine. Rory Finnin has been my mentor, colleague and friend from the very start of my academic career. The support extended by these people means more to me than I can express. I am very grateful to the inspiring writers Philippe Sands and Andrey Kurkov for contributing the foreword and the introduction to the book.

Three of the stories published in this volume appeared elsewhere in earlier versions: 'Army Boots' was published by *Krytyka*, 'A Ukrainian Obituary' and 'On the Edge of a European War, Who Gets to Defend the State' were published by *Open Democracy*. I'd like to thank the editors, Oleh Kotsyuba and Tom Rowley, for lending me their courage to deliver these texts to readers. I am grateful to Andreas Umland for his willingness to take on this manuscript and make it see the light of day in its first version. I extend my thanks to Jake Lingwood, Mala Sanghera-Warren and their team for giving this work a new life.

Most of all, I'd like to thank all those who made my brother's journey through the war a little more endurable, a little more humane. My gratitude extends to all who keep alive the memory of lives cut short by Russia's war in Ukraine.

UKRAINIAN VOICES

Collected by Andreas Umland

1   *Mychailo Wynnyckyj*
     Ukraine's Maidan, Russia's War
     A Chronicle and Analysis of the Revolution of Dignity
     With a foreword by Serhii Plokhy
     ISBN 978-3-8382-1327-9

2   *Olexander Hryb*
     Understanding Contemporary Ukrainian and Russian
     Nationalism
     The Post-Soviet Cossack Revival and Ukraine's National Security
     With a foreword by Vitali Vitaliev
     ISBN 978-3-8382-1377-4

3   *Marko Bojcun*
     Towards a Political Economy of Ukraine
     Selected Essays 1990–2015
     With a foreword by John-Paul Himka
     ISBN 978-3-8382-1368-2

4   *Volodymyr Yermolenko (ed.)*
     Ukraine in Histories and Stories
     Essays by Ukrainian Intellectuals
     With a preface by Peter Pomerantsev
     ISBN 978-3-8382-1456-6

5   *Mykola Riabchuk*
     At the Fence of Metternich's Garden
     Essays on Europe, Ukraine, and Europeanization
     ISBN 978-3-8382-1484-9

6   *Marta Dyczok*
     Ukraine Calling
     A Kaleidoscope from Hromadske Radio 2016–2019
     With a foreword by Andriy Kulykov
     ISBN 978-3-8382-1472-6

7   *Olexander Scherba*
     Ukraine vs. Darkness
     Undiplomatic Thoughts
     With a foreword by Adrian Karatnycky
     ISBN 978-3-8382-1501-3

8   *Olesya Yaremchuk*
     Our Others
     Stories of Ukrainian Diversity
     With a foreword by Ostap Slyvynsky
     Translated from the Ukrainian by Zenia Tompkins and Hanna Leliv
     ISBN 978-3-8382-1475-7

9   *Nataliya Gumenyuk*
     Die verlorene Insel
     Geschichten von der besetzten Krim
     Mit einem Vorwort von Alice Bota
     Aus dem Ukrainischen übersetzt von Johann Zajaczkowski
     ISBN 978-3-8382-1499-3

10   *Olena Stiazhkina*
     Zero Point Ukraine
     Four Essays on World War II
     Translated from the Ukrainian by Svitlana Kulinska
     ISBN 978-3-8382-1550-1

11   *Oleksii Sinchenko, Dmytro Stus, Leonid Finberg*
     (compilers)
     Ukrainian Dissidents
     An Anthology of Texts
     ISBN 978-3-8382-1551-8

12   *John-Paul Himka*
     Ukrainian Nationalists and the Holocaust
     OUN and UPA's Participation in the Destruction of Ukrainian
     Jewry, 1941–1944
     ISBN 978-3-8382-1548-8

13   *Andrey Demartino*
     False Mirrors
     The Weaponization of Social Media in Russia's Operation to
     Annex Crimea
     With a foreword by Oleksiy Danilov
     ISBN 978-3-8382-1533-4

14   *Svitlana Biedarieva (ed.)*
        Contemporary Ukrainian and Baltic Art
        Political and Social Perspectives, 1991–2021
        ISBN 978-3-8382-1526-6

15   *Olesya Khromeychuk*
        A Loss
        The Story of a Dead Soldier Told by His Sister
        With a foreword by Andrey Kurkov
        ISBN 978-3-8382-1570-9

16   *Marieluise Beck (Hg.)*
        Ukraine verstehen
        Auf den Spuren von Terror und Gewalt
        Mit einem Vorwort von Dmytro Kuleba
        ISBN 978-3-8382-1653-9

17   ·*Stanislav Aseyev*
        Heller Weg
        Geschichte eines Konzentrationslagers im Donbass 2017–2019
        Aus dem Russischen übersetzt von
        Martina Steis und Charis Haska
        ISBN 978-3-8382-1620-1

18   *Mykola Davydiuk*
        Wie funktioniert Putins Propaganda?
        Anmerkungen zum Informationskrieg des Kremls
        Aus dem Ukrainischen übersetzt von Christian Weise
        ISBN 978-3-8382-1628-7

19   *Olesya Yaremchuk*
        Unsere Anderen
        Geschichten ukrainischer Vielfalt
        Aus dem Ukrainischen übersetzt von Christian Weise
        ISBN 978-3-8382-1635-5

20   *Oleksandr Mykhed*
        „Dein Blut wird die Kohle tränken"
        Über die Ostukraine
        Aus dem Ukrainischen übersetzt von Simon Muschick
        und Dario Planert
        ISBN 978-3-8382-1648-5

21 *Vakhtang Kipiani (Hg.)*
    Der Zweite Weltkrieg in der Ukraine
    Geschichte und Lebensgeschichten
    Aus dem Ukrainischen übersetzt von Margarita Grinko
    ISBN 978-3-8382-1622-5

22 *Vakhtang Kipiani (ed.)*
    World War II, Uncontrived and Unredacted
    Testimonies from Ukraine
    Translated from the Ukrainian by Zenia Tompkins and Daisy Gibbons
    ISBN 978-3-8382-1621-8

23 *Dmytro Stus*
    Vasyl Stus
    Life in Creativity
    Translated from the Ukrainian by Ludmila Bachurina
    ISBN 978-3-8382-1631-7

24 *Vitalii Ogiienko (ed.)*
    The Holodomor and the Origins of the Soviet Man
    Reading the Testimony of Anastasia Lysyvets
    With forewords by Natalka Bilotserkivets and Serhy Yekelchyk
    Translated from the Ukrainian by Alla Parkhomenko and
    Alexander J. Motyl
    ISBN 978-3-8382-1616-4

25 *Vladislav Davidzon*
    Jewish-Ukrainian Relations and the Birth of a Political
    Nation
    Selected Writings 2013-2021
    With a foreword by Bernard-Henri Lévy
    ISBN 978-3-8382-1509-9

26 *Serhy Yekelchyk*
    Writing the Nation
    The Ukrainian Historical Profession in Independent Ukraine and
    the Diaspora
    ISBN 978-3-8382-1695-9

27 *Ildi Eperjesi, Oleksandr Kachura*
    Shreds of War
    Fates from the Donbas Frontline 2014-2019
    With a foreword by Olexiy Haran
    ISBN 978-3-8382-1680-5

28   *Oleksandr Melnyk*
World War II as an Identity Project
Historicism, Legitimacy Contests, and the (Re-)Construction of
Political Communities in Ukraine, 1939–1946
With a foreword by David R. Marples
ISBN 978-3-8382-1704-8

29   *Olesya Khromeychuk*
Ein Verlust
Die Geschichte eines gefallenen ukrainischen Soldaten,
erzählt von seiner Schwester
Mit einem Vorwort von Andrej Kurkow
Aus dem Englischen übersetzt von Lily Sophie
ISBN 978-3-8382-1770-3

30   *Tamara Martsenyuk, Tetiana Kostiuchenko (eds.)*
Russia's War in Ukraine 2022
Personal Experiences of Ukrainian Scholars
ISBN 978-3-8382-1757-4

31   *Ildikó Eperjesi, Oleksandr Kachura*
Shreds of War. Vol. 2
Fates from Crimea 2015–2022
With a foreword by Anton Shekhovtsov and an interview of
Oleh Sentsov
ISBN 978-3-8382-1780-2

32   *Yuriy Lukanov, Tetiana Pechonchik (eds.)*
The Press: How Russia destroyed Media Freedom in
Crimea
With a foreword by Taras Kuzio
ISBN 978-3-8382-1784-0

33   *Megan Buskey*
Ukraine Is Not Dead Yet
A Family Story of Exile and Return
ISBN 978-3-8382-1691-1

34   *Vira Ageyeva*
Behind the Scenes of the Empire
Essays on Cultural Relationships between Ukraine and Russia
ISBN 978-3-8382-1748-2

35   *Marieluise Beck (ed.)*
      Understanding Ukraine
      Tracing the Roots of Terror and Violence
      With a foreword by Dmytro Kuleba
      ISBN 978-3-8382-1773-4

36   *Olesya Khromeychuk*
      A·Loss
      The Story of a Dead Soldier Told by His Sister, 2nd edn.
      With a foreword by Philippe Sands
      With a preface by Andrii Kurkov
      ISBN 978-3-8382-1870-0

37   *Taras Kuzio, Stefan Jajecznyk-Kelman*
      Fascism and Genocide
      Russia's War Against Ukrainians
      ISBN 978-3-8382-1791-8

ibidem.eu